The Great Parade

Learning About Women, Justice, and the Church

Carol A. Wehrheim
Illustrated by Ethel Gold

FRIENDSHIP PRESS
NEW YORK

Contents

Introduction 3

Part 1: The Sessions

Session 1 Finding Images for God 6
Session 2 Created in the Image of God 10
Session 3 Images Gone Awry 13
Session 4 Women Leaders Around Us 17
Session 5 Women Who Made Big Changes 20
Session 6 The Gifts Women Share 23

Part 2: Stories and Activity Pages

Story 1: From All Sides 26
Story 2: So Different! 28
Story 3: Girls Restricted 30

Activity Page A: Ways We Can Talk About God 32
Activity Page B: Fair and Square 33
Activity Page C: Martha of Bethany 35
Activity Page D: Deborah 36
Activity Page E: Elizabeth Gurney Fry 37
Activity Page F: Susette and Susan La Flesche 38
Activity Page G: Lucy Maud Montgomery 39
Activity Page H: Yoshiko Uchida 40
Activity Page I: Esther 41
Activity Page J: Johnnetta Betsch Cole 43
Activity Page K: Priscilla 44
Activity Page L: Jane Addams 45
Activity Page M: Nellie McClung 47
Activity Page N: Dolores Huerta 48
Activity Page O: Corazon Cojuangco Aquino 49
Activity Page P: Miriam Wright Edelman 50
Activity Page Q: Women Who Led the Way 51

Part 3: Challenges

Challenge for Session 1 52
Challenge for Session 2 53
Challenge for Session 3 55
Challenge for Session 4 56
Challenge for Session 5 57
Challenge for Session 6 58

Bibliography 59

Hymns 60

ISBN 0-377-00244-5

© 1992 by Friendship Press, Inc.
Editorial Offices: 475 Riverside Drive, Room 860, New York, NY 10115
Distribution Offices: P.O. Box 37844, Cincinnati, OH 45222-0844

All rights reserved. No part of this book may be reproduced in any manner whatsoever without the written permission of Friendship Press, except for activity and challenge pages, which may be reproduced for class distribution.

Designer: Pat Achilles
Printed in the United States of America

Bible quotations in this book, unless otherwise indicated, are from the New Revised Standard Version, copyright 1989 by the Division of Education and Ministry of the National Council of the Churches of Christ in the U.S.A.

Library of Congress Cataloging-in-Publication Data

Wehrheim, Carol A.
    The great parade : learning about women, justice, and the church : with activity pages and teacher's guide / Carol A. Wehrheim.
      p. cm.
    Includes bibliographical references.
    ISBN 0-377-00244-5 : $7.95
    1. Women—Religious life—Juvenile literature. 2. Children—Religious life. 3. Christianity and justice—Juvenile literature. 4. Women—Biography—Juvenile literature. I. Title.
BV4527.W42 1992
261.8'344—dc20

91-43168
CIP

Introduction

Despite recent efforts to rethink traditional roles for men and women, we are painfully aware that we are not yet living so that "there is no longer male and female; for all of you are one in Christ Jesus" (Gal. 3:28). What we do or do not do to bring about that change will affect the world our children live in now and the one they will live in as adults. It is important that we make them aware of the need for justice for girls and women and help them see what part they can play in bringing it about.

ABOUT THIS BOOK

Because the history of women in the world and in the church is so well hidden, mission educators have developed this course of study for children as one small step toward uncovering it. The course is contained in this book, which is a teacher's resource. The title of the book, *The Great Parade*, is taken from the title of a hymn about God's people—men and women of all times and places. Book and course are an expression of "Churches in Solidarity with Women," the theme of the ecumenical decade 1988-1998. Together they are intended to help children and their teachers
- learn about national and global issues affecting women
- explore the diversity of images of God, especially in the Bible
- confront the difficulties and rewards of breaking down sexual stereotypes for girls and boys
- discover women who can be role models because they lived out their faith

Additional resources on this theme are listed on the inside of the back cover. A videotape, *Ashley and Adam* (described in Session 3), is also available.

As this book and course were developed, a question continually surfaced: What about the boys? Will they be left out of this course? The mission educators concluded that the course is an attempt to help both boys and girls understand that women, for many centuries, were denied equal participation in life of their communities and the mission of the church, and are often still so denied. In addition to learning about women, through the methods used in the course, based on cooperative education strategies, boys and girls will experience working and learning together as equal partners.

This book is divided in three parts. Part 1 contains outlines for six sessions for children in grades one through six. Part 2 consists of stories for the first three sessions and activity pages for all the sessions. Part 3 contains challenges appropriate to each session.

USING THIS BOOK

Part 1

You as the teacher should read through all the sessions first. Once you have a complete overview of the course, you will be better able to adapt it to fit your group and purposes.

Each session starts with a "Preparation" section, which includes the following elements:

- focus
- objective
- supplies
- scripture passages
- background reading
- things to do before the session starts

Then comes a "Class Activities" period, which follows a basic pattern.
- Arrival Time: activities that incorporate each child as he or she arrives and a review of the previous session
- Together Time: introduction to the focus of the session and related activities
- Work Time: working with the material just presented
- Worship: concluding song and prayers

Sometimes there will be additional elements such as "Story Time" or "Presentation Time."

Finally, there is a brief "Planning Ahead" session in which you evaluate the session and plan for the next one.

Part 2

The three stories, about boys and girls today, are for you to read and then tell to the children in the first three sessions. The activity pages, which are mostly short biographies of famous women in history, may be photocopied and given to each child. The instructions for using them are given in each session.

The symbol ▽ beside an activity indicates that it is more appropriate for younger children. The symbol ☐ indicates that the activity is more appropriate for older children. The final decision is up to you, of course, because you will know the abilities and interests of the children in your group. In addition, select the activities that will be most effective according to the time you have.

Part 3

"Challenges" suggest activities that adults and children can do together in the sessions or outside them. You may choose some of these activities to replace or augment those in the sessions. Even if you use some of them in class, it is recommended that you photocopy these pages to send home with the children. The total education of children regarding the role of women and girls in church and community cannot happen in six sessions but must be related to their daily lives. "Challenges" encourage parents and other adults who care about children to participate in this learning with the children.

If you plan as teachers to meet with parents and other adults, tell them about "Challenges." Talk about the important role they, as significant adults in the lives of the children, have in the success of this course. If you will not have an opportunity for such a meeting, consider a phone call to each home or a personal cover letter to be sent home with the challenge for Session 1.

ABOUT COOPERATIVE EDUCATION

This course has been designed around the concepts of cooperative education, a methodology that has existed for centuries but has only recently been studied by educators. Cooperative education recognizes that much of our life is based on cooperating with others to accomplish a task, whether in families, on the job, or in volunteer and leisure-time pursuits.

Many cooperative-education methods will be familiar to you. After all, education in the church, whatever the subject matter, is really about cooperation, where each person has an important role in working toward the good for the whole. As you adapt the session plans for your group, keep in mind these principles of cooperative education:
- Every child shares in the leading and learning. Together they are a whole.
- Each child is an integral part of the learning task. Each member of the group, or part of the body, is important.
- Direct interactions among the children are integral to learning and working together.

Cooperative education offers a valuable opportunity for teachers to work cooperatively, too. Remember to build in planning and evaluation time for gathering everyone who will be helping with this course. For more information on cooperative education, see the bibliography.

TALKING ABOUT GOD

Throughout this book you will find a variety of words used to talk about God. This variety is important for children, who take words quite literally. To use only masculine words or images for God leads children to assume that God is more like a man than a woman or that God is a man. Historically this assumption on the part of adults is one of the reasons that women have been kept from full participation in the activity of the church and even the community.

If you are not used to talking about God with many diferent kinds of words, or if you find it difficut to avoid referring to God exclusively by male pronouns, you will probably find this approach a little strange at first. You can be assured, however, that comfort will come with practice. If you would like to read more on this subject, see "Background" in Session 1 or the bibliography.

A FINAL WORD

Talking about the equality of men and women makes many of us feel uncomfortable at some point. We may like things as they are because as women we don't want to mow the lawn or as men we don't want to do the laundry. The ideal of equality in gender roles is not to change a person's preferences or a family's structure for accomplishing the necessary activities for life, but rather to insure that each person has a choice. The lawn must be mowed and the clothes must be washed. When these tasks are negotiated, rather than assigned by gender, the abilities and interests of each family member can be taken into account. (Unfortunately, this does not mean we don't have to do things we don't enjoy!) Often the choices are not recognized until we have seen examples, in ideas or practice. In this course, you and the children will be exposed to ideas, to practices, and to role models that will open up choices, both to equality and to solidarity. May you discover God's Spirit among you as you prepare and participate in this course.

PART 1

The Sessions

Session 1

Finding Images for God

PREPARATION

Focus

What is God like? How is God presented in the Bible? In what ways has the faith community through the ages tried to describe and understand God?

Objectives

To help the children
- find a working definition of "image" as a likeness of a person conveyed in words or pictures; it is not the same as the person but a representation of the person; it may represent many aspects of the person or one aspect
- discover some of the images that others use for describing God
- express their own ways of talking about God

Scripture Passages

Genesis 1:26-27 (creator); Deuteronomy 32:18 (one who gives birth); Psalm 23:1–3 (shepherd); 1 Samuel 2:2 (rock); Ruth 2:12 (wings of refuge); Psalm 31:1-5 (rock and fortress); Psalm 9:9-10 (stronghold for the oppressed); Psalm 27:1 (light); Psalm 68:5-6 (father of orphans and protector of widows); Jeremiah 18:6 (potter); Matthew 23:37 (hen with chickens); Luke 15:8–10 (woman who finds a lost coin)

	Supplies
Arrival Time	construction paper, markers, magazines to be cut up, scissors, glue
Together Time	Bibles, hand mirror, paper, pencils, newsprint pad and marker or chalkboard and chalk, index cards, Activity Page A
Work Time	construction paper, magazines for cutting, markers, scissors, glue
Worship	identity posters for God, poster with words for "Have We Not All One Loving God?"

Background

Language is a special gift to humanity, but it can also be limiting, as the child in the story "From All Sides" learns. When a single characteristic of a person is selected as the focus for identifying a person, other attributes of a person may be overlooked. This is often what happens when we focus on a single aspect of God.

How do you speak or think of God? Are there particular phrases or words that you use more than others? How do these favorite phrases enhance or limit your understanding of God? Although no one of us can fully understand God, we can regularly examine our language about God to see how we are limiting God by our speech. Yes, merely by attempting to describe God we limit God. We must be ever alert to what these limitations are. We limit our understanding of God when we ignore the warrior God or read only those psalms that present the forgiving character of God. By restricting our names or descriptions of God to one or two, we are rendering all other representations of God invisible. When only masculine pronouns and images are used for God, God seems to take on a male identity. Language about God is a difficult problem for theologians and Bible scholars, too. The future scholars who help us out of this difficulty may just be in your classroom.

In this session you and the children have an opportunity to add to the descriptions of God that you use in prayer and discussion. Increasing your knowledge of the words that can be used for God will also broaden your understanding of God. Because we have the gift of words to use, we can speak to one another about our faith as well as to God.

In Genesis 1:26-27, we learn that we are created in the image of God. Think for a moment about the ways we use the word *image* or refer to it in our everyday conversations. We say that she is the "spitting image" of her mother, or he "walks just like his brother," or "that whole family sounds alike." Rarely do we mean that we can't tell the persons apart. Rather, we see something in one that reminds us of the other. We might think of humans being created in God's image in the same way. What do we see in ourselves or others that reminds us of God?

Before You Teach

Take time to read and ponder the material in "Background" about your own image of God. Gather magazines with pictures of different races and cultures, for the children and you to make identity posters. Prepare your own identity poster or at least start it. Photocopy Activity Page A for the children. Gather the other materials listed on the supplies chart. Print the words to "Have We Not All One Loving God?" (page 61) on poster board or newsprint so the children can read them. On a large piece of newsprint or chalkboard, write the four directions for pairs of children reading scripture (page 8.) Learn this song if it is unfamiliar to you. Recruit someone to accompany the singing on a piano or guitar. If that is not possible and you feel uncertain about singing without accompaniment, ask a musician or the church choir to record the songs for this course on a cassette tape. Practice telling the story "From All Sides," so you can maintain eye contact with the children. Pray that God will use you to help the children glimpse a new image of their Creator.

Plan how you will use the challenge pages. See page 4 for suggestions.

CLASS ACTIVITIES

Arrival Time

➤ As the children arrive, direct them to the materials for making an identity poster. Using the construction paper as the background, each child is to create a poster that tells about herself or himself without using names or other words. They can cut pictures and pieces of pictures from the magazines you have provided. Some children may also want to add drawings of their own. Older children will probably want to work independently on their posters so others cannot see what they are creating. Younger children may need more direction. Suggest that they look for pictures of things they like to do. Finish your own identity poster if it's not completed.

As the children work, talk with them about their identity and their family. Ask

"What are some ways you are like others in your family?"

"Do you look like someone in your family?"

"Were you named for a relative?"

"Do people ever confuse you with a brother or sister?"

"Do they share your way of talking, stories or jokes?"

"What are some of the ways you are different from your family?"
(Remember that some children may not live in their families of birth.)

When all the children have finished their identity posters and joined you in conversation, you can move into the next activity.

Together Time

➤ Summarize what you have learned about the children from talking with them. For example, you might say, "I was surprised to learn that John was named after his great-grandfather. Did you learn something new about someone here?"

➤ Mix up the identity posters and spread them on the table or floor so everyone can see them. Warn the children not to let on which one is theirs. Selecting one poster at a time, have the children try to identify its creator. Invite each child to tell about her or his identity poster. If some children find it difficult to start on their own, be ready with a question, such as "What on your identity poster is your favorite thing to do?" When the children have finished, note the differences and similarities in what they have included.

➤ After all the posters have been identified or described, introduce the word *image*. Begin by asking the children to tell you what it means to them. Include in the discussion the ideas of "looking like, sounding like, acting like."

➤ To understand how people can be created in the image of God, we need to know all we can about God. The Bible is the book that the church has used for centuries to teach about God. It will be the primary source for the children in this session. If you have enough Bibles in the translation you have chosen, distribute them to the children. Ask them to find Genesis 1:26-27 in the Bible. If they seem uncertain, show them the table of contents. Find Genesis and explain that 1 is the chapter and 26 and 27 are the verses. Read the verses to the children. Older children may read them on their own. If you have not enough Bibles, ask an older child to help you find the verses and read them.

Ask the children: "What story are these two verses from?" (Most will recognize it as the story of creation.) Read verse 27 again, having the children listen for the word *image*. Ask them: "What is 'the image of God'?" (They may respond with "A picture" or "Made like God.") Follow up their answers with: "If we can't see or hear God, how can we tell that we are created in the image of God?" To help the children think about this question, ask one of the following questions to continue the conversation.

☐ Hold a hand mirror in front of a child and ask, "Whom do you see?" After he or she has named what is in the mirror, ask, "Is what you see the same as you?" The children may be better able to understand an image as a reflection, something like the thing reflected but still not the same as the reflected thing.

▽ Ask the children, "Has anyone ever told you that you look like or sound like or act like someone else? What do you think that person meant? Are you the same as the person you look or sound or act like?"

➤ ☐ Invite each child to choose a partner. If there is an odd number of children in the class, three children can work together. Have a child from each pair draw from a box or bowl one of the slips of paper with the Bible references. Go over with the children the following directions, which you have already written on the newsprint sheet or chalkboard:

1. One person in each pair finds the passage in the Bible.
2. The other person reads it out loud.
3. Both persons talk together about "What do these verses tell us about God?" One person writes the answer on an index card.
4. Both persons decide who will read their Bible passage to the total group and who will read the answer on the card.

When the children are ready, assemble them and have each pair read their passage and index card. Summarize each answer to the question in a few words or phrases and list them on newsprint.

After each pair has reported, read the list you have made to the children. This may be a good time to introduce the problem about using only male pronouns or descriptions in speaking of God. It is likely that the Bibles the children are using have only male pronouns in reference to God even though "he," "his," and "men" are not used generically. To help the children understand the problem, ask them what pictures come to mind when they hear the words *man, men, boy, his hat*. These words ordinarily bring a specific person or object to mind, not a general, non-gender-specific group. Also review "Background" (page 6) and "Talking About God" in the introduction (page 5). Other material on language about God can be found in the bibliography.

➤ Conclude "Together Time" by distributing copies of Activity Page A, "Ways We Can Talk About God," and having the children complete it.

☐ Have each pair of children select another pair to work with to list any other information they know about God. Provide them with paper and pencils. Have them complete the sentence, "God is . . ." as many times and in as many different ways as they can. Stop them after two minutes. Then have each team of four read their list. Add their information to the newsprint or chalkboard list you started earlier.

Ask the children: "Have we listed all there is to know about God?" They are not likely to say yes, but if they do, ask: "Do you think we can know all there is to know about God?" Comment on the different kinds of information or images of God that are listed, such as other names for God, things that remind us of God, or acts of God. Ask: "What do you think happens when we use only one or two of these words or phrases to think about or to talk to God?"

▽ Go over the questions on Activity Page A with the children. Encourage them to come up with other ideas.

Story Time

➤ To help the children think about the ways our images of a person or God can limit what we know about the person or God, tell Story 1, "From All Sides."

➤ Discuss the story, using the questions at the end.

Work Time

➤ ☐ Have the children work in the same teams of four they were in at the end of Together Time. The task of each team is to create an identity poster for God in the same way that the children created posters for themselves. Assign the following tasks to the team members: gather the materials from the supply table, keep the team on the topic, arrange the materials on the construction paper, watch the time as the team works on the poster. If there are five members on a team, a fifth task can be to name an image of God from their poster during the prayer as the group worships together. If there are teams with fewer than four members, combine the tasks. Encourage the children to review the information they have recalled and learned about God that you have listed on newsprint or chalkboard.

The teams who finish first can begin to learn "Have We Not All One Loving God?"

Worship

Place the identity posters for God in the center of the group as you did with the identity posters for the children. Have the children look at them in silence.

Sing "Have We Not All One Loving God?" The children who finished their posters first may be familiar with it. They can sing it to the group before everyone sings the song. Read together the song words you have printed on newsprint or posterboard before you sing it in unison.

Pray, using the format described here:

"God, we remember that you are more than we can imagine. Sometimes we think of you as _____."

"God, we thank you for creating us in your image. We are acting in your image when we _____."

(Repeat these sentences as often as necessary to have each team report.)

"God, help us to show your image to others through loving deeds. Amen."

Distribute Challenge for Session 1 for the children to take home, if you have chosen to use these pages in that way.

PLANNING AHEAD

Make notes about this session and how it went. Record comments about each child. You will find this information helpful as you plan Session 2. Look ahead to Sessions 4 and 5 to see what additional resources you might want to provide for the children.

Session 2

Created in the Image of God

PREPARATION

Focus
Being created in the image of God is what makes us unique as human beings.

Objectives
To help the children
- understand themselves as created in the image of God
- recognize the possibilities of differing gifts in themselves and others
- experience a way they can use their differing gifts to work together

Scripture Passages
Genesis 1:26-27; 1 Corinthians 12:4-6

Background
This session focuses on our being created in the image of God. We are not carbon copies or even machine copies of God or of one another. The image of God found in each of us comes from the same Spirit but is displayed in many ways and through specific gifts. We help others recognize an image of God through these gifts that God has given each of us. These gifts of the Spirit are the focus of this session. Think about each child in your class. What gift of God's Spirit does she or he bring to the group? How does this gift help others recognize God? Do the children recognize their own gifts? Do they value the gifts of their peers?

	Supplies
Arrival Time	index cards
Together Time	Bibles
Work Time	Bibles, puzzle or papers with words for Genesis 1:27, Activity Page A
Worship	Bibles

Because Christian speech and thoughts about God have traditionally been cast in masculine terms, the church has often overlooked the gifts that women have brought to God's mission on earth, or where it saw them, it often undervalued these gifts. This devaluation of women's gifts is not discussed explicitly in this session. Instead, the session will affirm the gifts of all persons, male and female, young and old, so the remaining sessions of the course can focus on the gifts and contributions of women.

Read 1 Corinthians 12 in its entirety for your own study and preparation to teach this session. Chapter 12 is often overlooked because it precedes the more famous chapter on love. Paul wrote chapters 12-14 because there was controversy in the Corinthian church about speaking in tongues. Some Corinthians claimed that the gift of tongues was a more important sign of God's Spirit than some other gifts, such as preaching or teaching. In chapter 12,

Paul points out that there are many types of gifts, but all come from God and should be used for the upbuilding of the body of Christ and to serve God. It is this point that is the focus for Session 2 with the children.

As you prepare for this session, think about the gifts from God that you are using. Thank God for them.

Before You Teach

Write on separate index cards all the images we use for God as compiled in Session 1. Make extra cards in case there are new children. Choose one of the games or activities under Work Time. Read through Story 2, "So Different."

CLASS ACTIVITIES

Arrival Time

➤ When the children arrive, tape an index card with one of the images of God on the back of each child. Do not let the child see what is written on the card. The children are to ask questions of others to determine which image of God is on the card on their back. Their questions should be answered with yes or no.

When a child figures out the image on the card he or she is wearing, the card can be taped to a bulletin board or placed on the table where you gather. The children who are finished can be available to answer the questions of those children who are still trying to solve the mystery of what is on their cards. Save the cards to use in Session 3.

➤ If space for moving is limited, an alternative to the activity above is a game similar to Twenty Questions. Have a child select a card and then answer the questions from the group as the rest of the children try to discover the image on the card. Since the children will have a sense of the range of answers, limit the number of questions to five.

If you used Activity Page A with the children in Session 1, cut the pictures from it to glue to index cards. This will work better if most of the children in the group do not read or are just beginning to learn to read.

Together Time

In Session 1 the focus was on the ways we talk about and think about God and how important it is to keep a variety of ways before us. In this session, the focus is on "male and female created in the image of God."

➤ When the children are settled in a circle on the floor or in chairs, distribute Bibles to them. Have them turn to Genesis 1:26-27. If some of the children are not sure how to find Genesis, ask other children to show them how to use the table of contents as described in Session 1.

☐ Read the two verses in unison. Then have half the group read verse 26 and the other half, verse 27. Ask such questions as: "What do you remember from our conversation about these verses yesterday? Look at them on the page. How are they different?" (Most Bibles print one verse as prose and one as poetry.) "Why do you think it is important that we are careful about how we talk about God?" (They might answer that God is special or important or powerful.) "Why is talking about God difficult?" (Their answers will vary depending upon what they understood from Session 1.) As you talk together help them come to the understanding that God is more than we can describe or even imagine.

▽ Show the children the verses in the Bible. Read each verse and have the children repeat it after you. Continue with the questions as above.

➤ Ask the children: "What image or idea of God might we see in ourselves or in others?" If the children have difficulty answering, have them look at the images from Activity Page A on the index cards. For example, if the description is a "rock," ask: "Does anyone support you like a rock? Are you ever a 'rock' for someone?"

▽ With younger children, choose the most concrete images that will help them make connections. You might ask: "Does anyone provide shelter for you the way the wings of a hen do for her chicks?" or "Is there someone who would look for you if you were the only one lost?"

▶ An alternative to this activity is an adaptation of the first activity on the Challenge for Session 2. Have each child draw a self-portrait on construction paper. Then, together, name ways that each child shows others some aspect of God's love. You can print these ways on the child's self-portrait as they are named.

Story Time
▶ Tell Story 2, "So Different." Discuss the story, using the questions at the end.

Work Time
▶ Begin this time with a discussion of 1 Corinthians 12:4-6. Distribute Bibles to the children and help them find this passage. Read it together. Ask them: "What kinds of gifts are we talking about here?" (abilities, skills, talents). "What are the services and activities?" (ways that we use our gifts to serve God and one another). Encourage the children to name specific things they can do. To help the children understand these verses, ask: "How does the story you just heard help you think about these verses?"

▶ As a change of pace and to introduce the topic of how different gifts of God can contribute to cooperation, play a game that requires the contribution of each child and teacher. Choose one of the games below, depending upon the size of your group and the ages and abilities of the children.

• Select a puzzle with the number of pieces roughly equivalent to the number of children in the group. The picture on the puzzle can be any object or scene, although you may want to look for a picture with children or a church building. If there are fewer children than puzzle pieces, other adults can join this game. If there are more children than puzzle pieces, ask for volunteers to be observers who will report on what helped the group do their task. Give each person one puzzle piece. There can be no talking. No person may take another person's puzzle piece. The group is to complete the puzzle.

When the puzzle is completed, ask the children what was helpful as they worked together and what was not. If there were observers, have them report first.

• Print each word of Genesis 1:27 on a separate piece of paper or index card. Have the group arrange themselves in order without talking. If the group is smaller than the number of words, use phrases. For a group of older children, include punctuation marks on separate cards.

Talk with the children about the game, using such questions as: "Was it hard not to tell someone else what to do?" "How could it have easier to solve the puzzle or complete the quotation?"

• As the children arrive, make a list of items that each one is wearing, looking for something that is unique to each child, for example, a tee shirt with Minnie Mouse or a sneaker with one broken shoelace. Print it where the children cannot see it and do not put any child's name on the list.

Have a human scavenger hunt by asking the group see how quickly they can find the items on the list you have created.

▶ If the games seem too easy for your group, pose a problem for them to resolve, such as "How can we keep the playgrounds cleaner?" or use a problem that you know is of particular importance to the children.

Assign a task to each child, such as making the list of possible solutions from the group discussion, listening so there are no put-downs, watching the clock, keeping the group on the subject, seeing that everyone has a chance to speak. Two children can be assigned the same or similar responsibilities. A larger group can be divided, but give each subgroup the same problem to resolve.

Conclude the activity by having the children state their solution(s). Have each child comment on how his or her task helped the group come to a conclusion.

Worship

Sing "Have We Not All One Loving God?"

Divide the group in three reading teams, assigning each one a verse from 1 Corinthians 12:4-6. After each verse is read by the assigned team, pause for silent or spoken prayers.

Read 1 Corinthians 12:4-6 to the children. Have them stand in a circle. Read the verses again. As you read the first part of each verse, the children point to each child around the circle. As you read the second part, they hold hands. Or you and the children can plan a way to use movement to show the meaning of these verses.

PLANNING AHEAD

Where did you notice signs of cooperation in the group today? Think about each child. When did she or he contribute to the work of the group? Look for images of God in others that you can use as examples with the children in the next session. Have you invited to your next session women from your community who hold positions traditionally held by men? Check to be sure your guests are coming and answer any questions they may have. Now that you know more about the group, you can suggest particular interests of the children.

Session 3

Images Gone Awry

PREPARATION

Focus

Although male and female were created equal in God's image, women and girls are often considered less important or less capable of participating in God's work than men and boys.

Objectives

To help the children
- recognize the negative portrayals of women and girls in Western culture
- evaluate these portrayals in light of our knowledge that all persons are created equal in God's image
- discover ways to counter negative portrayals

Scripture Passages

John 4:1-42; Genesis 1:27

Background

Children, both boys and girls, are very concerned about fairness. When they are helped to recognize acts of inequality, they begin to understand the need to redress such acts. As you plan and as you lead this session with the children, be alert to the feelings and prejudices they already have

	Supplies
Arrival Time	index cards from Session 2
Together Time	Bibles
Work Time	copies of Activity Page B, pencils, paper, markers
Worship	poster with words for "The Great Parade"

but are unaware of. A few sessions will not undo all the societal pressures and training they have already absorbed in their young lives, but a seed may be planted that will be nurtured by other persons and their experiences of faith. The stories of women who have worked for the rights of women in times when this was unpopular often reveal the impact of one story from the Bible or the influence of one adult in setting them on that course. Don't underestimate the importance of your task.

The story of the woman at the well from the Gospel of John presents us with many challenges. Jesus was clearly acting against the customs and norms of his day. Talking to a woman he did not know was most unusual, but talking to a Samaritan woman was even more out of the ordinary. Notice her amazement that Jesus, a Galilean, would ask her for water and the surprise of the disciples when they returned to find their leader talking seriously with a woman, a Samaritan women at that.

Read the whole story (John 4:1-42) for your own learning as you prepare this session. The meanings conveyed by water in this story are as wide and deep as the greatest ocean. Water, that liquid that keeps us alive. Jesus, the true water that gives us life. Jesus asked the woman first for water, but in the end he provided it for her. Put yourself in the place of the Samaritan woman. Try to capture her feelings at each juncture in the story. How do her feelings change? What change did this encounter bring to the community?

Before You Teach

Read and practice telling the story "Girls Restricted." Look over the Bible story and decide how much of it you will tell the children and how much of it they will read in Together Time.

Invite to this session one or two women in your community who work in fields that have traditionally been reserved for men, e.g., ministry, medicine, dentistry, fire fighting, police, piloting aircraft, truck driving, taxi driving, veterinary medicine, coaching football. You may also wish to invite a man who is working in a traditional women's field.

An alternative to having the guests in this session is to show the children the ten-minute video *Ashley and Adam,* which examines gender issues through the games that girls and boys play, the clothes that they wear, and the vocational aspirations of each sex.

Learn the song "The Great Parade" (page 60) and make a poster with the words.

CLASS ACTIVITIES

Arrival Time

➤ Tack the cards with the words or the pictures for images of God from Session 2 to a bulletin board that is accessible to the children or spread them out on a table or the floor with the children sitting in a circle around the cards. The group or circle can continue to grow if the children do not arrive at the same time.

Have the children think back over what happened in their lives since the last session. Ask: "When did you see people using their gifts from God this week?" You might start with an example, such as, "My neighbor helped me finish a birthday present so it would be ready on time."

▽ Younger children may find it easier to answer the question: "When did you see someone doing a loving act this week?" Encourage them to tell about loving acts of their own as well.

When the children have run out of examples or it is time to move to the next activity, summarize what they have been saying by pointing out the variety of gifts they observed and that both women and men, girls and boys, provided these glimpses of God working through them.

➤ To prepare for the discussion with the guests later in the session, tell the children that they will be talking with persons later about the kind of work they do for a living. Help the children decide what questions they will want to ask the guests, such as "How did you get your job?" "Why did you decide to do this?" "Are there times when you want to quit?" Print the questions on paper or index cards and distribute them to the children so they will have them when the time for the conversation comes.

Story Time

Tell Story 3, "Girls Restricted." If your congregation does not have acolytes, explain what they do before you tell the story. Feel free to change the story to make it more realistic for your listeners. Women who have not been permitted to hold church offices have found the same discrimination as the girl in the story.

➤ Discuss the story with the questions at its conclusion.

➤ An alternative to the discussion is to have the children act out the story. Older children can probably do this with ease after hearing the story once. Younger children may have more success if you tell the story again as they pantomime the actions.

Together Time

➤ The story was about a girl, but many women face discrimination in their jobs too. The guests you have invited to this session may have experiences of such discrimination. Ask them to talk about their experiences. Be sure the children are ready with questions to ask them. You may need to prompt them from time to time.

Then talk together about what a society misses when one segment of it is not able to work to capacity. Ask the children: "When women (or men) are not allowed to choose a career because they are women (or men), who loses out? What do women lose? What do men miss? What does society as a whole miss?" Invite your guests to contribute their insights into these questions too.

➤ To conclude this time, consider the story of Jesus and the woman at the well.

☐ Distribute Bibles to the children. Ask them to turn to John 4. If you do not have time to read verses 4 through 42, read verses 4 through 9, tell the story up to verse 27, and then read verses 27 through 30. Have the children follow in their Bibles as you or an older child reads.

▽ Tell the story to the group.

➤ To understand the surprising nature of what Jesus did here, the children will need to know something about women's roles and the treatment of women in the culture of Jesus' day. The older children may be aware of some of this information. Begin by asking them what they know about what women usually did in Bible times. Supplement their comments with the following information:

In Bible times, the most important role for a woman was to be a mother. Women who did not have children, who were considered "barren," believed that God was displeased with them. Therefore, women married at an early age and expected to be mothers quickly. Their husbands gave money, animals, or other items of value to the bride's father. The more important the family of the bride, the more was expected in this dowry.

Most women were confined to the home. They were expected to care for the family, venturing from their house or tent only to fetch water, sell their goods, or perform the necessary tasks of homemaking. They were not expected to discuss or take part in the work of religion, commerce, and education outside the home. Their husbands, brothers, or fathers made all major decisions for the family. The women and children were expected to follow these decisions. There are notable exceptions to this traditional role for women in the Bible, such as the prophetesses Huldah (2 Kings 22) and Deborah (Judges 4 and 5); Lydia (Acts 16), the seller of purple dyes: Priscilla (Acts 18), who taught about Jesus with her husband Aquila and Paul; and the women who traveled with Jesus as his disciples (Luke 8 and 23). But these were a tiny minority.

Girls were usually denied education. Their fathers took care of choosing husbands for them. When a girl married she might never see her family again, for now she belonged to the family of her husband. Women as well as men accepted this pattern as the norm. Clearly the lives of girls and women in Bible times were very different from the lives of girls and women in North America today.

As you conclude this activity, recall again the surprising things that happened in this story of Jesus and the woman at the well. She was a women he did not know, yet he asked her for a drink of water. She was a Samaritan women, a resident of a land that most Jews avoided entering. She was a woman who had had many husbands, another reason why Jesus might have avoided any conversation with her.

Work Time

➤ Since Bible times were different from today, the children need an opportunity to think about the roles expected of women and girls, boys and men, in the 1990s. To help them consider these roles and the meaning of equality, distribute Activity Page B for the children to complete on their own. (There is an Activity Page B for older children and one for younger children. If your group is mixed, have both available.)

After a couple of minutes, have each child find a partner so the two can combine their lists and add any other ideas.

Bring the children together and have them read their lists. Ask: "Why is equality important? What is needed for equality for women and girls today? What happens to men and boys when women and girls are granted equality? When they aren't granted equality?" Help the children see that equality for women and girls is a step to providing equality for everyone, including men and boys.

➤ Have the children, working alone or with others, create advertisements advocating equality for women and girls, thus for all. You may find that older boys rebel at preparing ads that talk about girls. In that case, suggest that they prepare ads that stress equality for all persons. Begin by talking about slogans they might use, such as the Chinese proverb, "Women hold up half the sky"; "male and female created in God's image" from Genesis 1:27; "many gifts, but all from God" from 1 Corinthians 12. Provide plain paper and markers for the children to use. Have pencils available so they can sketch out their designs before using the markers. As the children work, talk with them about their ads, encouraging them to ponder the need for pressing for equality for women and girls.

➤ Learn the song "The Great Parade."

Worship

Sing "The Great Parade." Another song that the children might know is "We Are the Church," which also describes an inclusive community of faith. It can be found in *Sing to God* (New York: United Church Press, 1984).

Invite the children to pray for equality.

PLANNING AHEAD

As a group, did the children begin to understand the unfairness of the treatment of women and girls in the past? Were the boys able to see that unless women and girls are treated fairly, they too have lost some of their equality? What from this session do you want to reinforce in Session 4?

Have you gathered information about women in your congregation or community who have worked or are working for peace and justice to use in Session 4 or 5? Although there are stories about such women in this course, learning about women the children know or may have heard of will help them recognize their own possibility of engaging in such work.

Session 4

Women Leaders Around Us

PREPARATION

Focus
For centuries most women have been discouraged from taking positions of leadership in congregations and communities throughout the world, but some outstanding women have been leaders.

Objectives
To help the children
- identify women in their communities and elsewhere who have worked or do work for justice, peace, and restoration of the integrity of creation
- recognize some of the barriers that women have had to fight against to gain equality
- plan ways to let others know of these women

Scripture Passages
Acts 9:36-42; 18:1-4, 18-28; Romans 16:3; 2 Timothy 4:19

Background
Although women have provided much help in churches as volunteers in the past, only in the last 40 years or so have most churches allowed them to take part in the major decisions of congregations and denominations. Even though the number of women clergy continues to grow, they still earn less than men and struggle to find positions where they can use their gifts and training. Just naming or electing women to governing boards of congregations has had a rough road, and there are still many groups of Christians around the world that do not permit women to hold such offices. Congregations have even withdrawn from denominations to avoid doing this. What is the history of your own congregation on this issue? What were or are the obstacles? Was it a smooth transition? Was there much turmoil?

	Supplies
Arrival Time	WomanWise poster or decade poster (see below)
Together Time	newsprint pad and marker or chalkboard and chalk
Story Time	Bible
Work Time	duplicated lists of women; Activity Pages C through I; pencils
Presentation Time	poster with words for "I Sing a Song of the Saints Today"
Worship	poster with words for "I Sing a Song of the Saints Today"

The children will probably not recognize the names of many women whose stories are on the Activity Pages (C-I) for this session. More important is that they recognize these names and contributions after the session is over. Feel free to add stories about women in your own congregation or community. Doing some research on your own will make the session even more interesting for you and the children.

Look over the activity using the stories about women in Work Time in this session and in Together Time and Work Time in Session 5. You may want to make a mural or prepare skits in both sessions rather than using each of those activities.

Before You Teach
Place the WomanWise poster (available from Friendship Press) in your teaching space or make a poster with these words: "Decade for Churches in Solidarity with Women—1988-1998." Learn "I Sing a Song of the Saints Today" (page 62). Make a poster with the words. Go over the Bible story about Dorcas. You may want to read it from a children's Bible storybook if your group is mostly younger children, or read the story

and tell it in your own words. Select the stories of women you will use from Activity Pages C through I. If you choose to send the entire set home with each child, make copies for each one. Duplicate a list of the names of these women along with the names of women from your congregation and community for whom you have complied information to use in Work Time.

CLASS ACTIVITIES

Arrival Time
➤ Invite the children to read the poster and see if they can figure out what it means. A hint for them is to think about the three previous sessions of this course. If any children were absent for the previous session, have those who were present tell them what you did and the important learnings from the session, especially the definition of "equality." This kind of review also provides you with a way to evaluate how the children understand what you have been doing together. This information can help you adjust activities and conversations so the learnings from this session can be connected to what they have already learned.

Together Time
➤ Introduce this period by saying something like the following: "One of the reasons for declaring the decade is to encourage women and women, boys and girls, to work so that women and girls will have what is already available for most men and boys. Solidarity means working together in such a way that all are equal. We sometimes say this in another way, such as working for peace and justice, or for peace and the integrity of the whole creation."

Have the children think about this question: "Who are persons in our church or community, today or in the past, who work so that all persons will have what they need to live?" No one is to raise a hand or answer until you give a signal. A good signal is to hold up an object that is used only for this purpose, such as a green circle or square. Restraining the opportunity to answer allows time for each child to think without the added pressure of hands waving in the air.

Invite the children to name such persons; as they do so, list them on newsprint or a chalkboard. When they have run out of suggestions or the time is up, have them look at the list. Ask: "How many are women? Men? How many are from the past? Today?"

If the children named fewer women than men, ask: "Why do you think there are so few women on the list?" If the number of men and women are about the same, say: "Not too many years ago when a list like this was put together, few persons would have thought to name women. Why do think that was so?" If there are more women, say: "We have mostly women on this list; are there more men that you can name?"

Story Time
➤ Divide the group by numbering off by twos. Tell the children they are going to hear or read a Bible story about Dorcas (Acts 9:36–42). The ones are to listen to the story with special attention to question 1 below. The twos are to listen with attention to question 2.
1. Why were Dorcas' friends so unhappy?
2. What was Dorcas known for doing for others?

Introduce the Bible story with the following: "All the way back to Bible times, women have worked for peace and fair treatment for all persons. This is a story about a women who lived about the time of Jesus."

▽ Read or tell the story to the younger children. Show them where it is found in the Bible. After the story, have the children make pairs, ones with twos. Instruct the children: "Tell your partner the question you had and the answer you found." Let them know that you will ask some of them to report what they learned to the whole group. They will need to listen carefully so that each one can report for the other person.

When everyone is ready, bring the group together. Ask one person to answer the first question. Check to see if all those who were listening for the answer agree or would like to add something to it. Follow the same procedure with the second question.

☐ Instead of telling the story, have the older children read Acts 9:32-43.

Have them make pairs and report their answers to each other.

Work Time

➤ This activity involves recognizing names on the list that you drew up in Together Time.

☐ Have the children remain in the same pairs. Give each pair a copy of the list and ask them to circle the names of the women they know something about. Then ask them to take turns telling the whole group what they know.

▽ Read the list of names to the children in a group. Help them identify the ones they know. Ask them to say something about the ones they have identified.

➤ In this activity the children will use Activity Pages C through I as the basis for skits.

☐ Ask the pairs of children to make teams of four. Give each team one of the Activity Pages C through I or a page that you have prepared with information about women working for peace and justice in your community. Explain that each team is to read its page together. Then it is to choose three things it wants the rest of the group to know about this woman and list them on the back of the page. Finally, each team is to plan a way to present this information to the group in a short skit. The skit can portray an incident in the life of the woman, be an interview with the woman, or be a conversation among the children about the woman.

▽ Select one or two Activity Pages C through I that the children can read easily or that you read or tell the group. Then they can work together on a skit.

➤ As an alternative to preparing a skit, the children can make a mural, as suggested in Session 5.

☐ Each team makes a mural.
▽ The whole group makes a mural.

➤ ☐ Some teams will probably finish their skit or mural before the others. Begin to teach them the song "I Sing a Song of the Saints Today." Explain to the children that the word *saints* in the New Testament refers to those who believed in Jesus Christ as in "calling the saints and widows" (Acts 9:41) and "as is fitting for the saints" (Rom. 16:2). This is the way it is used in this song too, for "saints" can also be used in that way today. Thus, each one of them can be a saint today.

Presentation Time

➤ Have each team or group present its skit. If there is time, sing together the first stanza of "I Sing a Song of the Saints Today" after each presentation.

Allow some time to talk about characteristics common to the women presented in the skits. Ask the children such questions as these: "Where did these women's ideas or concern for others come from? How was their faith or the church important to them? What difficulties do you think they encountered? Why do we remember them today?"

➤ Talk with the children about ways they can teach the congregation about the contributions of these women. They might consider the following ideas: create a bulletin board, prepare inserts for the church bulletin for three or four Sundays, present the skits at a congregational meeting or other event, create a word game using the women's names. You probably do not have time to work on the project in this session, but it can be the beginning project for Session 5.

Worship

Have everyone sing "I Sing a Song of the Saints Today" if the children did not sing it as they made their presentations. If there is not time to learn it, have the children read the words together from the poster you have prepared and plan to teach the song in Session 5.

Pray together by reading the name of each women presented by the children. Pause, after each name, allowing time for silent prayer or for the children to say prayers. Conclude by saying something like this: "God, who loves each person equally, help us to remember that we are equal in your sight and that you want peace and justice for all of us. Amen."

PLANNING AHEAD

Read and think through the major art project in Session 5. Plan now for a place to display it so the whole congregation can learn about these women. Take a few minutes to take stock of how the children are working together. If cooperative education is new to them, they may have some difficulty believing that you want them to work as a team to complete the task. Look back at the information about cooperative education in the introduction. Review the theory behind this method of education so you can evaluate the way you have used it and plan to use it more effectively.

Session Five

Women Who Made Big Changes

PEPARATION

Focus

In spite of discrimination, many women have become national and international leaders, working for peace and justice for all.

Objectives

To help children
- identify women who have been or are champions of peace, justice, and the integrity of creation on a national or global scale
- praise women who work for peace, justice, or the integrity of creation
- prepare a display to tell others about some of these women

Scripture Passages

Esther 1-10; Acts 18:1–3, 18, 24–28

Background

Many women over the years have not only influenced the people in their communities but have also worked to bring justice and equality to persons, especially women and children, throughout their nation or the world. The women discussed in this session have all done so, in various ways and with differing gifts. Remember, though, that women throughout history were generally

	Supplies
Arrival time	photocopies of the list of women from Session 4, pencils
Together Time	World map or globe
Work Time	Activity Pages J through P; scrap paper; pencils; art supplies such as crayons, markers, colored chalk, construction paper, magazines, scraps of colored and textured paper, yarn; glue; scissors; large index card (5" x 7"); large sheet of construction paper, poster board or shelf paper
Presentation Time	mural panels from each work team; masking tape or tacks
Worship	poster with words for "I Sing a Song of the Saints Today"

prevented from exerting this kind of influence. Too often the stories of those who were leaders have not been included in the history texts, but a little searching in your public library will reveal more of them to you.

Although some of the women the children will study in this session were denied access to official church positions, they were women who maintained a connection to the church or faith community. This faith sustained them as they worked for their own rights and the rights of others. Both boys and girls can take this important lesson from these women. If there is a woman in your congregation or community who has played an important role in gaining justice for others on a national or global basis, invite her to talk with the children. Tell your guest what the group has been doing and how you think she can contribute to their experience of this course.

Before You Teach

Make clean copies of the list of women presented in Session 4. Photocopy Activity Sheets J through O, enough for each child if you plan to send the entire set home with him or her. Plan teams of two or three for Work Time and duplicate the list of directions for them (see page 21) or print them on a newsprint pad. Gather the supplies for the murals.

CLASS ACTIVITIES

Arrival Time

➤ Give the children clean copies of the list of women you made in Session 4. If a child was absent, have him or her work with a child who was present. Ask the children to read the list and circle the names that they recognize and can describe to someone else. Have the children tell one another about the woman or women they learned about in the previous session.

As they finish the review activity, help the children work on the plan they chose to tell the congregation about the women from Session 4.

Together Time

➤ Introduce the focus for this session by having the children name ways that women have worked for peace, justice, and the integrity of creation, calling again upon their work in Session 4. The children who presented each woman can determine whether the information given is adequate and correct.

Explain that in this session they will learn about women who have worked for peace and justice either nationally or globally. Many of the women they learned about in Session 4 influenced others beyond their community, but they tended to focus their attention on their own community. Name the women for whom you have information on Activity Pages J through P, saying a few words about each one.

Explain briefly that the women they will learn about in this session were known beyond their community or region. On a world map or globe, help the children locate your town or city. Then find the state or province, nation, and continent on which you live. Although young children are just developing some map skills, this visual description will help them see the wider impact of those who influence a region larger than their own community or city.

Work Time

➤ In this period the children will use stories of women given in Activities Pages J through P to make a mural.

☐ Each of the teams you have formed is to read an activity page and prepare one panel of the mural. If the class includes a wide range of ages of children, be sure each team includes children who read and write well along with those whose reading and writing skills are less developed.

By this time you have some idea of the abilities of each child and can assign these tasks: bringing supplies, reading to the team, and making the mural. The responsibilities can be divided or grouped according to the size of the team. A team of more than five, however, generally does not work well. Remind the children that although each has a particular task, each one is responsible to help in developing the final mural. Have them read the following instructions that you have duplicated for each team or written on newsprint.

1. One person brings supplies from the supply table and also brings the infor-

mation from the teacher about a woman.
2. One person reads the activity page to the team.
3. The scribe writes down things that are important for the team to remember about the woman. Other team members may suggest what this information is. Notes can be just a word or two because you can refer back to the activity page.
3. Together decide which information you want to include in a paragraph about the woman, which will be posted with your panel for the mural. The scribe prints the paragraph on scrap paper first so it can be checked with the entire team. When it is satisfactory, the scribe transfers it to the large index card.
4. Together decide what you want in the picture about the woman on the mural panel and what supplies you want to use. One person is responsible for making the mural, but everyone helps make it.
5. When you have completed your mural panel and the index card, return any extra supplies to the supply table and together clean up your work space.
6. Decide who will read the information on the index card to the group when you present your panel.

▽ Select one or two stories from the activity pages and read them to the whole class. Help them decide what information to use and write it for them, but allow them to do most of the work on the mural themselves.

Presentation Time
► Assemble the teams and have each team add its panel to the mural and read the information on the index card to the group. Or read the card you helped the younger children prepare. Encourage the children to ask questions of one another. Write down questions for which the information is not available. Suggest that they ask their parents or other adults about these women. Perhaps they (or a teacher) can look for this additional information before the next session.

Worship
Sing together "I Sing a Song of the Saints Today."

Pray the following responsive prayer. Print the response on newsprint or chalkboard and read it together two or three times before you begin the prayer.

Leader: Creator God, who gave both women and men the responsibility of caring for your creation and all who live in it, hear our prayers.

For (name of one woman)

Response: Thank you, God, for her life and work.

(Repeat for all the women in the presentation.)

Leader: We honor these women who have shown us the way to care for others. Amen.

PLANNING AHEAD

Which women did the children remember from Session 4? Are the plans for presenting this information to the congregation complete? As you think about each child, which women have made an impression on each one? The next session concludes this study. Look over the plan. How will you adapt it so the children in your class will leave with a sense of achievement and completion?

Session 6

The Gifts Women Share

PREPARATION

Focus
We celebrate the many gifts that women use in working toward the vision of God's justice, peace, and the integrity of creation.

Objectives
To help the children
- honor the gifts of women
- summarize the learnings of this course
- acknowledge their own potential to work for peace, justice, and the integrity of creation

Scripture Passages
Genesis 1:26–27; 1 Corinthians 12:4–6

Background
No new content is introduced here, but the children have the opportunity to assimilate what they have learned into their own lives. Adapt this session to include any activities that you brought to the session plans. Make it a time of joy.

Let the children know how much you enjoyed this time with them. Perhaps you can plan a way to check with them in a few weeks to see how much everyone is working for equality and justice.

Before You Teach
Look through the activity pages about the women the children have studied so you have an idea of the eras when they lived. Gather supplies, such as colored paper, artificial flowers, and strips of cloth, for the children to create the worship center for the closing segment of the session. Duplicate Activity Page Q for children to work on as they wait for others to be ready for the celebration, or to complete at home. Learn "Come Let Us Honor Those Who Led the Way" (page 64) and make a poster with the words.

Supplies

Arrival Time	index cards with the words of Genesis 1:26-27; Bible
Together Time	shelf paper or other paper for the time line; markers; Activity Pages B–0
Work Time	poster with words for "I Sing a Song of the Saints Today"; chalkboard and chalk; newsprint and markers; flowers, cloth, mural from Session 5, and other items for worship center; posters with words for "Come, Let Us Honor Those Who Led the Way" and "The Great Parade"
Worship	posters with words for "I Sing a Song of the Saints Today" and "Come, Let Us Honor Those Who Led the Way"; Bible; items prepared by the teams in Work Time

CLASS ACTIVITIES

Arrival Time
► Hide around the room the cards that you made for the game with Genesis 1:26-27 in Session 2. As the children arrive, have them look for the cards and bring them to the table. If all the children have arrived and there are still cards hidden, invite the children to continue the search.

When all the cards are found, the children can arrange them in the order of verses 26 and 27. To check their work, a child can find the verses in the Bible.

Together Time
► To help the children recall each woman discussed in Sessions 4 and 5 and to gain a sense of the many years over which women have worked for the integrity of creation, peace, and justice, make a time line.

At the left margin of a 3-to-4-foot length of paper, write "Old Testament Times." At the right margin, write this year's date. Print each woman's name, contribution, and known birth and death dates in the proper place, allowing plenty of space for the 19th century. Ask each child to select the woman he or she likes best and tell in what way he or she would like to resemble her.

This activity can be expanded by having children draw small pictures of events in the life of each woman and attaching them to her name with yarn, string, or tape.

Work Time

Depending on the size of the group, the number of tasks to prepare the closing celebration will vary. Create a team of two to four children to accomplish each task. A group of five or less may have two teams or may work together. Select tasks from the descriptions below, adding any that you think will be particularly meaningful to your group.

▶ Have a team write additional stanzas to "I Sing a Song of the Saints Today" about selected women or more generally about the search for equality, peace, and justice for women. To help the children keep the rhythm of the song, draw spaces on a chalkboard (easily erased) representing each note or syllable of the lines of the stanza. For example, the first line would look like this:

— — — — — — — — — —

Note that the last three syllables can be tied together, as in the first stanza.

To begin, have the children list words or phrases to incorporate into the stanza. Make sentences and try singing them to the music. They may need further refinement to make them fit the music

When everyone is satisfied, copy the new stanza on newsprint so everyone can see it and sing it during the closing celebration.

▶ Have the team learn "Come, Let Us Honor Those Who Led the Way." After you have read the first stanza together, ask the children to identify the women described in it. Priscilla or Lydia, perhaps, Esther and Deborah. Sing the first stanza together. Read the second stanza and talk about women who would fit the description in it, such as Nellie McClung and Jane Addams. Sing the second stanza together. Finally read the third stanza and talk about ways you can work for wholeness of the church. Sing the entire song.

▶ Have the team create prayers for the celebration. Through the course the children have been involved in various kinds of prayer—sentence prayers, litanies, and prayers to which they added their own words. Help them recall these ways to pray. This prayer will focus on women included in the course and our commitment to follow their footsteps as workers for equality, peace, and justice.

Have the children select a format for the prayer and write it together. See the following example, writing a sentence for each woman studied or others the children want to include. Then have the team decide whether they will read the prayer in unison or different members will read different sections.

Spirit of God, Creator of us all, we remember the women who have followed you and led us to this day. We honor their lives and pray that we might follow their example.

For Susette and Susan La Flesche, who fought courageously for their people the Omahas,

We give you thanks, Ruler of the Universe.

▶ Have a team prepare a worship center for the celebration. A focus for the worship time will help them center their attention on God. Have the team name some things that symbolize this course for them. The worship center can be objects assembled from those you have gathered, the mural they created in Session 5, or a drawing that this team creates. This team can also be responsible for arranging the space for the worship celebration.

▶ Have a team prepare a call to worship to open their worship together and a benediction to close it. The team may write these pieces or select one of those below:

Call to Worship

Come boys, come girls, created in God's image. Let us worship our creator.

Come worship God, who shepherds us and shields us, one and all.

You were created in God's image, come and worship the one who keeps you in the wings of refuge.

Benediction

Lead us from death to life
from falsehood to truth.
Lead us from despair to hope
from fear to trust.
Let peace fill our hearts
our world, our universe.
Let us dream together,
pray together,
work together,
to build one world
of peace and justice
for all.

Reprinted from *Ecumenical Decade 1988-1998 Churches in Solidarity with Women: Prayers & Poems—Songs & Stories* (p. 31) 1988 WCC Publication, World Council of Churches, Geneva, Switzerland.

Together Time

▶ Talk with the children about ways they have worked, including learning, for peace and justice for women and girls during these lessons. Reinforce the understanding that in working for justice for women and girls, justice for men and boys is also insured and increased. Help the children plan ways that they can continue to act for the integrity of creation, peace, and justice.

Worship

Worship together, using the parts of worship prepared by the children. You may follow the order given or one you and the children devise.

Call to Worship
Song: "I Sing a Song of the Saints Today," including stanzas written by the team
Scripture: 1 Corinthians 12:4-6
Prayers
Song: "Come, Let Us Honor Those Who Led the Way"
Time of Commitment: Have the children name something they will try to do or think quietly about it.
Song: "The Great Parade"
Benediction

Begin with, "Let peace fill our hearts." Conclude with, "Go now in peace, rejoicing in the love of God, who created you and will ever sustain you." Finally tell them, "We have ended this learning time together. Remember what you have learned. Be happy that God loves you and will always love you."

As the children leave, be sure they take with them any art work, activity pages, or challenge pages left from other sessions.

EVALUATING THE COURSE

The task of teaching is not complete until you have taken a few moments to think back over the sessions and how they went. Ask yourself these questions:
- What was the most exciting moment of the course?
- Which was the least exciting moment?
- Which children gained the most from the course?
- How did each child grow as a result?
- Which children seemed untouched? Why?
- How did you grow as you taught? In faith? As a teacher?

PART 2
Stories and Activity Pages

STORY 1
From All Sides

Susan flopped down on the porch swing.

"I hate those kids," she muttered. "They're awful and stupid. I don't want to play with them anyway."

The baby sitter came to the door.

"I thought I heard a noise out here. What's wrong? You look like the world is about to end."

"Don't care if it does."

Trish opened the door and sat down beside Susan. Bet she's never been called "Fattie," thought Susan. Trish was 16 and lived down the street. She was staying with Susan during the day while mother was at her office.

"Want to talk about it?" Trish asked.

In a shaking voice, Susan told Trish about the kids at the swimming pool making fun of her and calling her "Fattie" and "Whale."

Susan was relieved that Trish didn't try to tell her it would all be okay. It wouldn't! Even though she didn't want to return to the pool, she knew she wanted to learn to swim and that would mean going back to the pool tomorrow morning.

When her mother came home, she asked Susan, just as she did every day, "How did it go today, dear?"

Susan hadn't planned to say anything about the kids at the pool. Before she knew it she was crying and talking and her mother was hugging her.

"I know it is cruel for them to tease you. I wish they would take time to find out all about you. What would you like them to know about you?"

"Nothing!" Susan said at first. After a moment, she added, "That I am not afraid of snakes. Or spiders."

"Right, and that you know some really funny riddles. One of these days maybe they will be able to learn these things about you. Concentrate on the swimming for now. They'll get tired of teasing you if you ignore them. They'll soon see that you're there to learn to swim just the way they are."

After dinner, Susan and her mother played two of Susan's favorite games. This was a special treat in the summer when there was no homework. Then they read a story from the Bible. It was really two stories because it told about a shepherd who lost one sheep and a woman who lost one coin (Luke 15:3-10). Jesus told the stories in order to help people understand God's plan for creation, for women and men, for girls and boys.

Later, as Susan prayed before going to sleep, she thought of the stories. One story wasn't enough to learn about God. Jesus told many stories, each one a little different.

As she lay in bed looking at the stars shining so brightly in the dark sky, she thought about the kids at the pool. Why can't they see that I am more than the way I look? she wondered. They don't even know that I like to paint or that I can wiggle my ears. Don't they know that it takes more than one story to get to know some one?

TO DISCUSS
- If you were Susan, what would you do at the pool the next day?
- Suppose you were one of the kids at the pool. Deep down you didn't feel very good about teasing Susan. What would you do the next day?
- How do we get to know more about a person?

STORY 2

So Different!

Mei and Emi looked exactly alike. Their hair was exactly alike—black as licorice. Their eyes were exactly alike—dark and sparkling. They were exactly the same height—4 feet, 1/2 inch. They weighted exactly the same—59 pounds. When you saw them on the street, you could not tell them apart. They were identical twins.

If you watched them at school, however, it didn't take long to tell Emi from Mei. Emi loved to be around friends. She was always getting into trouble for talking during silent reading time. Mei liked her friends, but she liked best to do things by herself or only with Emi. She never got into trouble for talking during silent reading.

This year in the fourth grade, Mei and Emi were interested in very different activities. For the first time, both girls did not select the same subjects during the special January week when they could choose from a zillion topics. Emi talked with her friends to see what they wanted to do. They all decided to sign up for drama and for storytelling. Mei looked at the list for several days. Finally she decided to register for signing, a language that uses hand signs instead of spoken words. She chose it because she had seen a woman at church sign for the worshipers who couldn't hear. Her choice for the second subject was poetry writing.

The girls enjoyed their subjects. The drama group prepared a play and presented it to the whole school. It was so good that they presented it again one evening to parents. Emi had the biggest part in it.

Mei was a little sad that Emi spent so much time with her friends. She and Emi used to do everything together. It was hard not to have Emi around to get things going. To be truthful, she also felt a little jealous of Emi. Emi had drawn lots of attention because of the play. Nobody even asked to see one of Mei's poems.

In April a new girl joined the fourth grade. She seemed very quiet and shy. Before she came, the teacher explained that the new girl couldn't hear very well. She had to watch people's lips carefully to understand what they were saying. The teacher asked everyone to help the new girl by speaking clearly and standing so she could see their faces.

TO DISCUSS
- What do you think happened next?
- What gift did Emi have? Mei?
- How are your gifts different from those of your brother, sister, or friend?

STORY 3

Girls Restricted

Gretchen watched every move her older brother made as he carefully lit the candles in the front of the sanctuary. Today was the first Sunday for him to serve as acolyte for the service of worship. Ryan had gone to special classes to learn about the service and how to light the candles. When I am 13, I am going to be an acolyte too, Gretchen promised herself.

For a long time she kept this promise tightly inside herself. One day when she and her best friend, Jenna, were talking about their church, she told Jenna, "In two more years I am going to the classes so I can be an acolyte."

Jenna actually laughed in her face. "An acolyte? You're a girl. Girls can't be acolytes."

Gretchen's face turned red with anger. "Why not? What's so hard about lighting candles?"

"I don't know what's so hard about it," replied Jenna, speaking more seriously, "but have you ever seen a girl acolyte?"

Gretchen was silent. No, she had not seen a girl serve as acolyte. Could there really be a rule against it?

Gretchen and Jenna didn't talk about acolytes again. Gretchen didn't tell her secret dream to anyone. She hardly dared think about it herself, but she didn't forget it.

Nearly two years later, Gretchen saw an announcement in the church bulletin that a class for acolytes was to begin. The announcement read: "Children 13 years and older are invited to become acolytes. The classes will be held for five weeks on Wednesdays after school."

At dinner that Sunday, Gretchen was unusually quiet. Finally she said, "I would like to go to the classes for acolytes." Then she held her breath.

"Gretchen, only boys are acolytes," said Ryan. He didn't laugh in her face, but he did make her feel a little foolish.

Her mother and father looked at each other. Gretchen knew that look. This would call for a conversation between them before they would say anything to her. The subject was dropped.

That night, both parents came to her room after she was in bed. She knew what that meant too—time for a serious discussion.

"Gretchen," her mother began, "we would like for you to be an acolyte, too. However, Ryan is right in that there have never been girl acolytes in our congregation."

Her father said, "We believe that girls have the right to be acolytes, and the notice did say 'children'."

"Tomorrow you may call the church and ask if you may attend," promised her mother. "But Pastor Becker is new. She doesn't know that we have not had girl acolytes. I can't promise you anything."

Gretchen could hardly wait to get home from school the next day. She hurried in the door, looking for her mother. She really didn't want to call unless her mother was nearby to help her out. She didn't know Pastor Becker, although the pastor was always very friendly.

TO DISCUSS

- Did anything about this story surprise you? What?
- What argument do you think persons might have used to say that girls could not be acolytes:
- What argument would you use to say that the girls should be treated equally as the boys?
- Are there things in your church that boys can do but girls cannot? What are they?
- Have you ever experienced discrimination? What happened? What did you do?

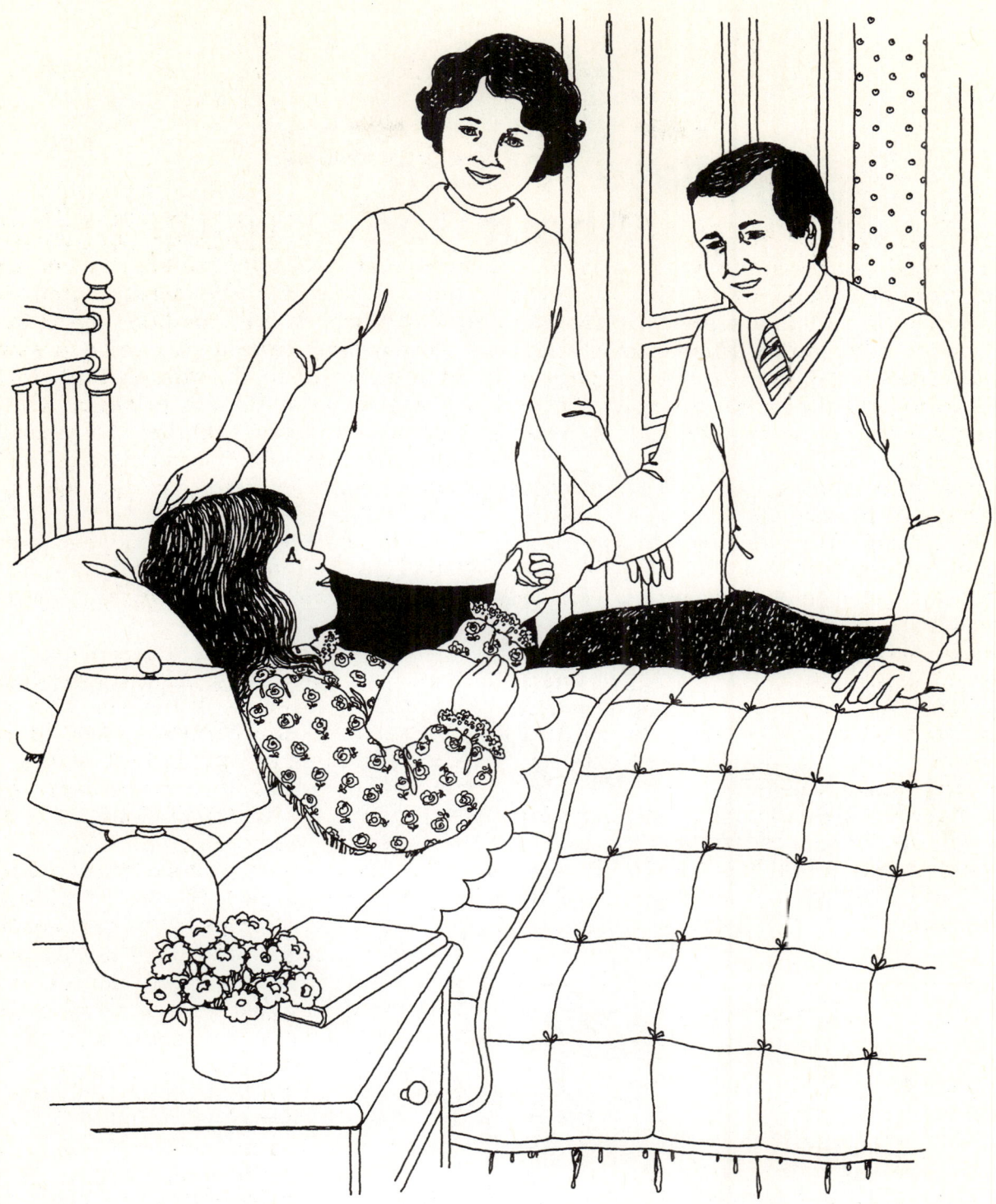

When Gretchen hung up the phone, her mother was right there to hear what had happened.

"Well," began Gretchen. "Pastor Becker said she thinks that girls have as much right to be acolytes as boys. But because she is new, she is going to talk about it with the Worship Committee tonight. She will let me know."

Pastor Becker must have known how much Gretchen wanted to be an acolyte. When the meeting was over, she called and told Gretchen that it was all set. She was welcome to come to the classes.

ACTIVITY PAGE
A

Ways We Can Talk About God

Look at the pictures. They are ways we can describe what God is and does. Draw a line from each picture to the words that describe it.

potter

hen sheltering chicks with wings

light

shepherd

rock

fortress

ACTIVITY PAGE
B ☐

Fair and Square

Equality: being equal in rank, amount, size, etc.; with no advantage on one side; one does not control the other

Which of these examples describe equality?
. . . Only those who are good batters can play softball.
. . . All children are invited to try out for the swim team.
. . . Boys cannot take cooking classes.
. . . Girls cannot enter the relay.

In the space below write the meaning of equality in your own words. You can write a story, a paragraph, or a poem.

ACTIVITY PAGE B ▽

Fair and Square

Which pictures show the persons being fair?

Tell a friend what equality means to you.

ACTIVITY PAGE
C

Martha of Bethany
Friend of Jesus

Lived in Bethany near Jerusalem, early first century A.D. Death date unknown.

Martha, her sister, Mary, and their brother, Lazarus, were close friends of Jesus. From the Gospel of Luke (10:38–41), we have this story:

Jesus came to their home. Mary sat down to listen to him talk. Martha busied herself with preparing the meal. With so much work, she was angry that Mary was not helping her. She asked Jesus, "Don't you care that my sister is not helping to prepare the meal?" He said to her, "Mary has chosen the better thing for now, to hear what I have to say."

But Martha too knew the importance of Jesus. We have another story about their family in the Gospel of John (11:1–44):

Their brother, Lazarus, was very ill. The sisters sent word to Jesus, hoping that he could heal his good friend, Lazarus. When Jesus finally arrived in Bethany, Lazarus had been dead for four days. Martha greeted him, "If you had been here, Lazarus would not have died. But God will do whatever you ask." Then she made an important statement, "I believe that you are the one sent by God for whom we are waiting."

Mary greeted Jesus with sobs and complained, "If you had come sooner, you could have saved him."

Jesus saw the sorrow of the sisters and their friends. He felt his own sorrow. Then he had them roll the stone away from the grave, and Lazarus walked out alive.

In the Gospel of John we also learn that Mary rubbed Jesus' feet with expensive oil the night before he was taken a prisoner. She and Martha recognized the importance of Jesus long before his other followers did.

These two sisters had considerable money and were known throughout their community. It is likely that Martha was the older and that she was an excellent homemaker. No doubt people admired her faith as well.

Martha was admired for centuries after she lived, too. In 1300 a famous preacher wrote about Martha that she was the ideal of the woman who acts carefully and who works for the best for everyone. During the Middle Ages, many pictures of Martha appeared that portrayed her strong faith. Legends developed about her. A popular one was that she had killed the dragon representing evil. Perhaps you know the story of St. George and the dragon. Many churches then had pictures of both George and Martha and the dragons they had killed.

Based on Luke 10:38-42; John 11:1-44; and Elisabeth Moltmann-Wendel, *The Women Around Jesus* (New York: Crossroad, 1982).

ACTIVITY PAGE
D

Deborah

Prophetess for the Israelites

Lived in Ephraim between Ramah and Bethel about 1100 B.C.E.
Death date unknown.

Deborah stood up slowly from her seat under the palm trees on the hill. She was waiting for the warrior Barak. She had a special message for him. She knew he would come, for as a prophetess she was respected by all the Israelites. They often came to this palm tree between Ramah and Bethel in the country of Ephraim to seek her counsel and advice.

When Barak came, she said to him, "Take 10,000 men. Go to Mount Tabor. Meet the mighty Sisera and his army. God will be with you and you will win."

Barak knew that Sisera had many soldiers, surely more than he had. "Deborah," he said, "I will do this only if you will go with me."

Deborah agreed, but she said, "A woman, not you, will get credit for the victory over Sisera."

Barak and Deborah did meet the army of Sisera. Barak and his soldiers defeated the army, but Sisera escaped.

When Sisera saw that his army was beaten, he ran to the tent of Jael. She invited him inside and said, "Do not be afraid. Have some food and drink."

Sisera ate and relaxed. He was very tired and fell asleep, thinking that he was safe. When he was sound asleep, Jael killed him.

Later Barak came looking for Sisera. Jael took him into her tent and showed him Sisera. Then he knew that Deborah's words were true. The victory over Sisera would go to a woman.

Following the victory, Deborah and Barak sang a song of praise to God that told the story of the victory. Then there was peace in the land for 40 years, for Deborah was a wise counselor and judge, faithful to God and her people.

Based on Judges 4 and 5 and Edith Deen, *All of the Women in the Bible* (New York: Harper & Row, Publishers, 1955).

ACTIVITY PAGE
E

Elizabeth Gurney Fry
Pioneer in prison reform

Born: May 21, 1780, in Norwich, England.
Died: 1845.

Many years ago people who broke the law were almost always put in prison. Women, men, girls, boys—all were placed in the same building, sometimes the same big cell. The food was moldy and rotten. The space was too cold or too hot, and it was dirty. If a mother was sent to prison, her children went with her.

Most people paid little attention to the prisons. One Quaker woman, Elizabeth Fry, did pay attention to them. Even as a child, Elizabeth was kind to everyone. She thought things through and made a decision about them that she stuck with. She thought about the prisons and she made a decision that she stuck with.

When Elizabeth Fry learned about the terrible conditions in Newgate Prison in London, near where she lived, she began to visit there to try to help the women.

At first the guards and people in charge did not want to let her in. "Go home to your family," she was told. But Elizabeth Fry had made her decision and she was determined. Finally a guard opened the door.

At first the women didn't trust her. She was dressed in fine clothes. What did she want with them?

Week after week Elizabeth Fry returned with food, medicine, and clothes. Then she began to teach the women to sew and to read. She brought her friends with her. They scrubbed floors and windows. They formed a special group to work for changes in the prisons. They called the group the Association for Improvement of the Female Prisoners in Newgate.

Elizabeth Fry didn't stop with helping at Newgate. In 1818 she and her brother visited prisons in Scotland and northern England. The notes she took during this trip were published. They made her work famous around the world. She was invited to visit prisons in France, Switzerland, and Belgium.

And Elizabeth Fry didn't stop with helping those who were imprisoned because they had done something wrong. She also worked for the improvement of conditions for those who were called insane.

Elizabeth Fry was married to Joseph Fry and had several children. Still she found time to visit those in prison, just as the Bible tells us to do, and she encouraged many others to do so too.

Based on Jan Johnson, *Angel of the Prison* (Minneapolis: Winston Press, 1977) and the *Encyclopedia Britannica*, 1973.

Susette born: 1854 on the Omaha reservation, Nebraska. Died: 1903.

ACTIVITY PAGE
F

Susette and Susan La Flesche

Omaha women who worked for the welfare of their people

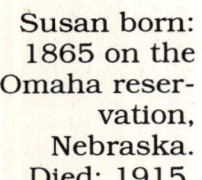

Susan born: 1865 on the Omaha reservation, Nebraska. Died: 1915.

Susette La Flesche was the oldest daughter of Mary and Chief Iron Eye (Joseph La Flesch) of the Omaha tribe in Nebraska. Susan was their youngest daughter. Both girls went to the mission school on the reservation, and then went East to the Elizabeth Institute in Elizabeth, New Jersey. Both served the Omahas all their lives.

Susette returned to the reservation to teach. Since her older brother Louis had died, her father discussed tribal maters with her. When the U.S. government treated the Omahas and their relatives the Poncas unfairly, Susette translated for her father during the conferences with government officials.

When the Poncas were forced to move from their land, Susette learned that neither they nor the Omahas had any rights. They weren't counted as people in the U.S. Constitution. She wrote of this treatment to Thomas Tibbles, an editor at the Omaha *World-Tribune*, who published her story exactly as she had written it.

From then on the paper regularly published the news of the Poncas and Omahas. Susette (known as Bright Eyes), her brother Francis, and Thomas Tibbles toured the East telling of the unfair treatment of the tribes. After several years of their hard work, Congress passed bills to allow the Poncas to return to their land and later to the Omahas to negotiate a title for their land. During those years, Mrs. Tibbles died, and Thomas and Susette married. She took over the care of his daughters and wrote stories of Indian life.

Susan was an outstanding student. After Elizabeth Seminary, she went to Hampton Institute in Virginia, where she received a gold medal for scholastic achievement. Then she went to the Women's Medical College in Philadelphia, where she graduated at the head of her class.

After a period of internship at Women's Hospital in Philadelphia, she returned to the Omaha reservation to be the doctor at the mission school. She married Henry Picotte, but that did not prevent her becoming the doctor for the entire reservation. Each night a light shone brightly in her front window so those who needed help could find her. She also served as medical missionary for the Presbyterian Board of Home Missions and, like her sister, spoke out for her people.

Based on Margaret Crary, *Susette Laflesche: Voice of the Omaha Indians* (New York: Hawthorne Books, 1973) and Marion E. Gridley *American Indian Women* (New York: Hawthorne Books, 1974).

ACTIVITY PAGE
G

Lucy Maud Montgomery
Writer and minister's wife

Born: November 30, 1874, in Clifton, Prince Edward Island. Died: 1942.

Maud was less than two years old when her mother died. She went to live with her grandparents in Cavendish, Prince Edward Island. She had few playmates in the country, but she created two imaginary ones in her reflections in glass bookcase doors. She named them Katy Maurice and Lucy Gray.

Maud wrote poetry and stories as a child. She continued to write, sometimes getting up very early, as she attended college and then worked as a teacher and for a newspaper. Although she sent her writing to various magazines and newspapers, all she received were letters of rejection.

When her grandfather died, she returned to Cavendish to care for her grandmother. By that time (1889) she was receiving some money for her writing. By 1901 she was making a "liveable" income from it. Still, most manuscripts were rejected.

Throughout her life, Maud was active in the Presbyterian church. In a book about her life, *The Alpine Path*, she wrote:

> We liked the Sunday School much better than the church services. Some of my sweetest memories are of the hours spent in that old church with my little mates, with our testaments and lesson sheets held in our cotton-gloved hands. Saturday night we had been made learn our catechism and our Golden texts and our paraphrases [of Bible texts]. I always enjoyed reciting those paraphrases, particularly any that had dramatic lines.

As an adult she regularly taught Sunday school classes. It is not surprising, then, that she became secretly engaged to the pastor of the church in Cavendish, Ewan Macdonald. They knew that they could not be married as long as she cared for her grandmother. During this time she wrote her most famous book, *Anne of Green Gables,* set in the Cavendish area that she loved.

When she married Ewan in 1911, she moved to Leaskdale, Ontario, where he was now pastor. After a three-month honeymoon in the British Isles, she returned home and did all that was expected of the minister's wife. She also continued to write. Many books later she became a Fellow of the Royal Society of Arts in England, the first Canadian woman to receive this honor. She was also invested with the Order of the British Empire.

The land around Cavendish, which especially inspired her writing, was made into a national park in 1936.

Based on L. M. Montgomery, *The Alpine Path*, 1917 (Reprinted Markham, Ont.: Fitzhenry & Whiteside, Ltd., 1990) and Mollie Gillen, *Lucy Maud Montgomery* (Markham, Ont.: Fitzhenry & Whiteside, Ltd., 1978).

ACTIVITY PAGE
H

Yoshiko Uchida

Writer of children's books

Born: November 24, 1921, in Alameda, California.

When Yoshiko was 10 years old, she and her family traveled from California to Connecticut to visit friends. There she first learned about prejudice. People assumed that she was not a citizen of the United States but had been born in Japan. At 16 at the University of California, Berkeley, again she met prejudice, for the only social club she could join was one for Japanese Americans.

In 1942 her life changed drastically. Japan attacked the United States, and war was declared. People became suspicious of anyone who looked Japanese, whether the person had been born in Japan or not. People of Japanese descent were ordered to leave their homes and were sent to prisoner-of-war camps.

The Uchida family had just 10 days to sell their home and sell or store their possessions, except for what they would carry. Their camp was at the Tantaren Race Track in Montana. They were among 8,000 Japanese Americans who lived in the stables and barracks there. They were assigned a stall about 10 feet by 20 feet. In this dirty, smelly, poorly lit space, they found three army cots, no other furniture. Nevertheless, the Uchidas helped organize schools, churches, and recreation centers. Yoshiko taught the second grade.

Five months later, they were transferred to Topaz in the Utah desert. This camp was no better than the race track. Each barracks had six rooms to house six families. Heavy dust storms covered every space with grit and choked the prisoners.

Yoshiko attended Smith College in 1943. When the war ended in 1945, the Uchidas returned to a more normal life, but Yoshiko could never erase these years from her memories. Years later she used them to write stories for children. In *Journey Home* the mother says, "How can I pack our whole life into boxes and cartons in just ten days?" Sure Yoshiko and her mother said these words.

When Yoshiko talks with children about her books, she always asks them why they think she wrote the books. During the conversation, a child always answers, "So it will never happen again." Yoshiko nods and smiles.

Based on Ann Commire, ed. *Something About the Author*, vol. 53, 1988, and Yoshiko Uchida, *Journey Home* (New York: Atheneum, 1978).

ACTIVITY PAGE
1

Esther

Jewish queen of Persia

Lived in Susa in Persia (modern Iran) in 400 B.C.E. Death date unknown.

Mordecai, a Jew living in Susa, hurried his cousin and adopted daughter, Esther, to gather her things to go to the court. King Xerxes was looking for a new queen, a beautiful queen to replace Queen Vashti. Vashti had not obeyed his command, and so was no longer his queen.

When Esther arrived at the court, she and the other young women who had also come prepared themselves for a year to meet the king. Then the king chose Esther to be his new queen. Mordecai was made an assistant to the king. The king did not know, however, that they were Jews.

As time went on, the prime minister, Haman, was angered because Mordecai would not bow down to him. When other officials urged him to do so, Mordecai said, "I am a Jew. I cannot bow to Haman, only to God."

Haman was furious. He convinced the king to send an order throughout the land that all Jews should be killed on a certain day. When Esther learned of this she was very sad. Mordecai warned her, "Do not think you are safe because you live in the palace."

Esther sent word to all the Jews in the land to pray and fast for three days so that she might know how to help her people.

No one, not even Queen Esther, was allowed to go before the king unless the king asked to see that person. Esther dressed in her finest clothes and walked back and forth in the courtyard outside the throne room. Finally the king sent for her. "What do you want, Esther? Ask and you shall have it."

"If it would please Your Majesty, I would like you and Haman to come to a banquet tonight."

They came. Haman was certain he was gaining favor with the king and queen. At the end of the banquet, King Xerxes said, "Tell me what you want, Queen Esther, and I will grant it."

"I wish," replied Esther, "that you and Haman would come tomorrow night for another banquet."

That night Haman began to plot for the death of Mordecai. Meanwhile the king had a book about his life read to him. When he heard about the time that Mordecai had saved his life, he asked, "What did I do for that man?"

The answer was, "Nothing." The king sent for Haman and asked him, "How should I show honor to someone?"

"Dress him in your finest robes. Set him on your finest horse and take him through the streets. Have a nobleman announce, 'See how the king rewards a man he wishes to honor!'" Haman was sure he was the man the king wanted to honor.

The king and Haman came to the banquet prepared by Queen Esther on the second night. Again, the king asked,

Based on the Book of Esther.

"What can I do for you? I will do anything."

This time Esther said, "My wish is that my people will live. A command has gone out that they are all to die."

"Who gave such a command?" inquired the king.

"Our enemy, Haman."

The king was furious. He ordered Haman hanged. Sadly, the king told Esther that once a royal decree had been issued, it could not be taken back. He could not save her people. However, he allowed Esther and Mordecai to issue any decree they wished, under the king's name.

Their decree was that the Jews could defend themselves. As it happened, the Persians became very frightened of the Jews when they knew the Jews could fight them. The Jews destroyed their enemies and thus were saved.

From that time on, the Jews tell the story of Queen Esther who saved her people, when they celebrate Purim, on March 14 and 15 of every year.

Johnnetta Betsch Cole

First black woman president of Spelman College

Born: October 19, 1936, in Jacksonville, Florida.

Johnnetta's parents were both college graduates. Her father was a successful insurance man, respected by the entire community. Johnnetta was a star pupil in school, including being the double-Dutch jump-roping champion when she was a young girl.

When she was 15 Johnnetta left Florida for Oberlin College in Ohio. Although her father wanted her to enter the insurance business, she found anthropology more to her liking. She went on to Northwestern University to learn more about anthropology.

In 1960 she met and married Robert Cole, who was white. When he came to meet her parents in Jacksonville, they received threatening phone calls. Two years later Johnnetta and Robert went to Liberia on a research team. It was an exciting time.

As time went on, Johnnetta had three sons. When she was offered a teaching job at the University of Massachusetts in Amherst, the family moved there. Her husband was not able to find a permanent job. Eventually he left and they were divorced.

Johnnetta Cole had no intention of being a college president, but Spelman College, in Atlanta, Georgia, a school begun for black women, sought her out. She became president in 1986. There she is able to be a role model for the students, who call her "Sister President." She has also been able to improve the school, bringing other black women to the faculty. Today Spelman is usually named among the best private schools in the United States.

When she was a child, Johnnetta was told to stand up straight and to speak up, Johnetta Cole stands tall today and speaks out for the rights of women and men. For all she has accomplished, she was awarded the 1991 Achievement Award by the American Association of University Women.

Based on Mary Catherine Bateson, *Composing a Life* (New York: New American Library, Plume Books, 1990) and "Sister President, Johnetta Cole," *American Association of University Women Outlook*, April/May 1991.

ACTIVITY PAGE
K

Priscilla

Teacher in the early church

Lived in Rome and Corinth in the first century A.D. Death date unknown.

I'm so sorry to leave Rome, Priscilla thought as she packed the few things she and Aquila, her husband, would take with them. Claudius, the ruler of Rome, had said that all Jews must leave the city. There was nothing they could do but pack their tent-making tools along with a few household goods and leave.

They had spent a long time talking about where to go. They knew that they wanted to go where there were people who followed Jesus. Finally they chose Corinth, in Greece.

When they arrived in Corinth, they quickly made themselves known to the Christians there. In no time they were leaders, and a group of Christians often met in their home.

They were delighted when the apostle Paul came to visit the church in Corinth. He stayed with them for he was a tent maker too. They worked together and talked about Jesus. How much they learned from him! Priscilla wanted to know everything that Paul knew.

Evidently Paul thought that she did know, for he took them with him to Ephesus (in modern Turkey) and left them there to establish the church he began.

While they were there a Jew named Apollos came to the city. He knew many teachings of the scriptures. However, when Priscilla and Aquila heard him, they realized that he did not know what they knew of Jesus the Christ. Priscilla invited him to stay in their home. There she and Aquila taught Apollos all that they knew about Jesus the Christ.

Paul did not forget about Priscilla and Aquila as he traveled. When he wrote to the Christians in Corinth, he especially remembered the church that met in their home. When he wrote to Timothy, he asked him to greet them for him. When he wrote to the church in Rome, he named them as two who had risked their lives for him.

Priscilla was probably better known than Aquila. Her name is found in other histories of the period. For a woman to be mentioned so often in the Bible and in such a positive way, she must have been outstanding. There was even one catacomb, a place where the early church gathered to worship in secret, named in her honor.

Based on Acts 18:1–4; 18:18–28; Romans 16:3–4; 1 Corinthians 16:19; 2 Timothy 4:19 and Edith Deen *All of the Women in the Bible* (New York: Harper & Row, Publishers, 1955).

ACTIVITY PAGE
L

Jane Addams

Founder of Hull House and pioneer for child labor laws

Born: September 6, 1860, in Cedarville, Illinois. Died: 1935.

Jane's mother died before Jane was two. She loved and admired her father throughout her life. He was a highly respected legislator in Illinois, known for his honesty. Each week he taught Sunday school and Jane accompanied him. He also made sure that she was aware that not all children had the clothes and other things that she did and that she ought not to show off what she had when she was around them.

Jane went to Rockford Seminary, a school for young women where the students were encouraged either to go into missionary work or to marry. Jane did neither. When she was graduated she was at loose ends, not sure what to do with her life.

Shortly after that her father died. Jane enrolled in the Women's Medical College in Philadelphia because she had promised him she would do so. Although her grades were good during the first semester, she knew that medicine was not her field and left the school.

She and her friend Ellen Starr traveled to Europe. There they saw many poor people. They also toured a settlement house, a building where poor persons could come to learn trades, make friends, and become better educated. Jane and Ellen returned to Chicago determined to begin a settlement house there.

They ended up on Halsted Street, in a neighborhood filled with new immigrants from Europe. The buildings were old and crowded, and the streets were dirty. None of the houses were connected to the city sewer system.

They searched for the right building until they discovered Hull House. The owner, Helen Culver, gave it to them rent free. They were on their way! They cleaned it and furnished it with the furniture from Jane's home.

Hull House was a school where there were courses in art, music, cooking, and dressmaking. Hull House was also a clubhouse, with groups for men, women, boys, and girls. There were special groups, such as a Shakespeare Club and the Women Necktie Workers Club. Hull House gave money to those who were in need and found jobs for those who were unemployed. There were public lectures on Thursday nights and concerts on Sunday afternoons. A kindergarten was begun, and child care was provided for working mothers. The Jane Club was set up, a boarding residence for 50 young women.

Jane and Ellen joined Fourth Presbyterian Church. Following in her father's foot-

Based on Hope Stoddard, *Famous American Women* (New York: Thomas Y. Crowell Co., 1970) and Mary Kittredge, *Jane Addams, Social Worker* (New York: Chelsea House Publishers, 1988).

steps, Jane taught a Sunday school class. Through the church she made many wealthy friends who helped her support Hull House and who volunteered there with her. By the end of the first year, 20 volunteers lived at the house, and many more came daily or weekly. To Jane this proved her belief that the poor and rich classes needed each other.

One night Jane Addams found a robber in Hull House. Imagine his surprise when she questioned him. "What are you doing here?" The man explained that he was out of work and had a family to feed. She told him to return the next day. When the man did, she already had found a job for him.

Because the city did not collect garbage regularly, Jane applied to be the garbage removal agent for the neighborhood. Her bid was thrown out, but she was appointed garbage inspector of the ward. During her term, workers dug through eight inches of refuse to unearth pavement on one street. The death rate in the ward was lowered from third to seventh in the city.

Another area of concern for Jane was child labor. Young children worked in factories and other dangerous places. Jane spoke to many groups around the city, urging restrictions on child labor. She is credited for some of earliest laws protecting children. She was also interested in education, women's right to vote, and the end of war.

In 1931 Jane Addams was awarded the Nobel Peace Prize, her most treasured honor. She could not attend the ceremony because she was hospitalized for surgery. The award drew attention to her legacy: the establishment of settlement houses and child labor laws.

ACTIVITY PAGE
M

Nellie McClung

Author and worker for women's rights

Born: 1874 in Ontario. Died: 1951.

Nellie was the youngest of six children, but she didn't hang behind any of them when it came to determination. When she was six, her family moved to a farm in Manitoba. There each child had specific work to do. Her father and the boys worked in the fields and on the buildings. Her mother and the girls tended the garden, milked the cows, sewed all their clothes, and prepared all the food.

When Nellie was tending the cattle on the range with her dog, Nap, she would sit and think. She thought about the way the boys were allowed to do some things that she wasn't, even when she knew she could run races or ask questions or make decisions as well as they could.

When Nellie was 16, she went away to Normal School to train as a teacher. Her first job was to teach all eight grades at the small town of Somerset. Some of the older students were bigger than she was! Unlike other teachers, she took both boys and girls outside to play football, and she played with them!

Nellie was a good teacher, but she felt that teaching was not what God wanted her to do. Often she lay awake in bed asking: Why do some people think women shouldn't be educated? Why are women not allowed to take some jobs? Why can't women vote? Why isn't it against the law for a husband to beat his wife? Why don't women do something about this?

The night came when Nellie knew that God wanted her to find ways to change these injustices, to make it fair for women. Fairness was very important to Nellie. She didn't forget this task, not even when she married Wesley McClung and had five children. She worked as hard as she had on the farm to win the same rights for women that men had. Although many men and women spoke against her, she convinced many people that the vote for women was fair. Through her efforts a law was passed in Manitoba in 1916 giving women the right to vote in that province.

Still concerned about fairness, Nellie was elected to the Alberta Parliament in 1921. In 1936 she became the first woman on the Board of the Canadian Broadcasting Corporation. She also wrote 16 books, including *Clearing in the West* and *The Stream Ran Fast* about her life, as well as short stories and poems.

Based on Tom McCarthy, *Nellie McClung, The Girl Who Liked to Ask Questions*. (Ottawa: St. Paul University, Novalis, n.d.).

ACTIVITY PAGE
N

Dolores Huerta

Organizer of farm workers

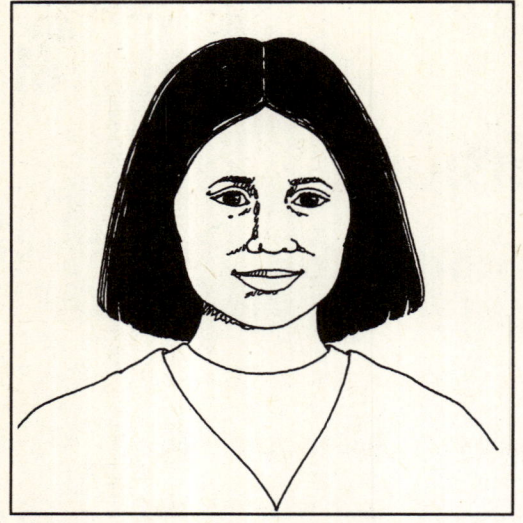

Born: April 10, 1930, in Dawson, New Mexico.

Dolores moved often with her Mexican American family as they followed the harvest of crops in California. When her parents divorced, she, her two brothers, and her mother settled in Stockton. They lived in a neighborhood where there were Chinese, Latinos, Native Americans, blacks, Japanese, Italians—nearly every ethnic group you could imagine. Dolores joined the Girl Scouts and sang in the church choir. Her best friend was Chinese and Buddhist. They enjoyed learning about each other's religion and background.

In high school, though, she learned about racism. In one class, she received A's on all tests and papers, but she got a C for the course. The teacher said that the work was too good and surely someone else had done the writing for her. She sold the most war bonds, but she was not awarded the trophy because she was Mexican American. She was on a committee to plan a dance. One person said that if they didn't charge $3 admission people would think the band wasn't any good. Dolores knew there were many boys and girls who could not afford to pay $3. She resigned from the committee when they would not lower the fee. Even then she stood up for the rights of others.

Dolores' mother ran a hotel that housed farm workers. There Dolores learned firsthand about the poor working conditions in the fields and how the workers were often cheated. She never forgot these people. Years later, she joined the Community Service Organization (CSO). There she met Fred Ross, whom she married and who changed her life. She worked on voter-registration drives. She became a lobbyist and spoke to government groups, asking for laws that would benefit farm workers.

In 1962 she left CSO to help Cesar Chavez organize a union for migrant farm workers. She held the highest job of any woman in the organization. She divorced Fred Ross, and married Ventura Huerta. In her work she traveled often, but the farm worker organization was like a big family. Her children were never alone.

She marched in the first grape strike in 1965. Then she organized a boycott against grapes for the East Coast. On behalf of farm workers, she testified before Congress and talked to all kinds of groups, soliciting their support. A reporter asked her how she would like to be remembered. She replied: "I would like to be viewed as a women who cares for fellow humans. We must use our lives to make the world a better place, not just to acquire things. That is what we are put on earth for."

Based on Janet Morey and Wendy Dunn, *Famous Mexican-Americans*. (New York: Dutton, Cobblehill Books, 1989).

ACTIVITY PAGE
O

Corazon Cojuangco Aquino

Born: January 25, 1933, near Manila in the Philippine Islands.

One of six children of a well-to-do family, Corazon was educated in Roman Catholic schools in the Philippines and in the United States. After a year of studying law at Far Eastern University in Manila, she married Benigo Aquino, Jr., known as Ninoy. Almost at once, he became active in political affairs. Although he won the election for mayor of Concepcion, he was not allowed to take office because he was too young. At 35 he was the youngest senator in the history of the Philippines.

When Ferdinand Marcos was elected president of the Philippines, he took away basic rights of the people, Ninoy spoke out against these practices and was jailed in 1972. Corazon, quiet and soft-spoken, argued with officials to find out where he was and to gain permission to visit him. As time went by, Ninoy became ill. Corazon faced officials once more to insist that her husband be flown to the United States for surgery. Her request was granted.

For a few years Ninoy, Corazon, and their five children lived peacefully in Massachusetts, where Ninoy was studying and teaching. He was not happy, however. He believed that he must return home to fight Marcos. Although great care was taken to arrange his trip secretly, he was shot dead as he left the plane in Manila.

Now it was Corazon who was in the center of the political activity. Over a million persons signed papers asking her to run for president. Marcos surprised everyone by calling for an election, probably because he thought he could not lose.

Elections in those years were run by Marcos and his friends. The United States sent observers to see that fair elections were held. Finally Corazon Aquino was declared the winner. Marcos left the Philippines.

The days ahead were difficult for the new president. There were rumors that she would be forced out of office, even killed. One of her most difficult tasks was to prepare a new constitution. In 1987 it was put before the people for a vote. Nearly every eligible voter came to the polls. The constitution was accepted by 76 percent of the voters. This meant that Corazon Aquino would be president for six more years, until a new election.

Life has not been easy for Corazon Aquino and her family. But they have worked together and for their country, trying to bring fairness to each person's life.

Based on Laurie Nadell, *Corazon Aquino: Journey to Power* (New York: Julian Messner, 1987).

ACTIVITY PAGE
P

Marian Wright Edelman

Civil rights worker and founder of the Children's Defense Fund

Born: June 6, 1939, Bennetsville, South Carolina.

In Bennetsville as a child, Marian could not play on the public playground or eat at the drugstore lunch counter. Black people weren't allowed there. So her father, a Baptist minister, build a playground and a snack shop behind the church where everyone was welcome.

Whenever Marian's father saw a problem or need, he tried to do something about it. This is the model that Marian has followed ever since. She learned at an early age that doing well meant to be helpful to others, to achieve in school, and to read everything you could find. She and her four brothers and sisters worked hard at these things.

Marian was 14 when her father died. She was with him at the end. He reminded her that she, a young black girl, could be and do anything. Marian has proved him right.

Marian went to Spelman College, where she was active in the civil rights movement. She worked to assure blacks of voting privileges and access to public places, such as playgrounds and restaurants. She graduated in 1960.

While working for voters' rights, Marian decided that to make a real difference she should become a lawyer. She went to Yale Law School. During school vacations she continued to work for civil rights.

Through her work she came to see the great need for good education for all children. She worked for programs for poor young children in Mississippi. She made many trips to Washington to tell senators and representatives what the children needed. Sometimes they came to Mississippi to see the problem for themselves. That was how she met her husband, Peter Edelman, who was an aide to Senator Robert Kennedy.

Marian decided to move to Washington in 1968 to be closer to where the decisions were made and also to marry Peter.

In 1973 she began the Children's Defense Fund, an organization that lobbies for all children but especially poor children. Even today, although she has three sons, Marian Wright Edelman is concerned about every child in the United States of America. The lesson she learned as a child, that serving others is as much as part of life as sleeping or eating, is one that she teaches by example today.

Based on Calvin Tomkins, "A Sense of Urgency" in *The New Yorker*, March 27, 1989 and *The State of America's Children 1991* (Washington, D.C.: The Children's Defense Fund).

ACTIVITY PAGE
Q

Women Who Led the Way

She opened Hull House. _ _ _ _ _ _
She is president of a college. _ _ _ _
She wrote *Anne of Green Gables*. _ _ _ _ _ _ _ _ _ _
She saved her people. _ _ _ _ _ _
She helped women get the vote. _ _ _ _ _ _ _
She taught Apollos. _ _ _ _ _ _ _ _ _
She is president of a nation. _ _ _ _ _ _
She helped people in prison. _ _ _

Find their names in the letters below.

```
C  A  C  A  D  D  A  M  S  Q  P  O  D
O  E  M  O  N  T  G  O  M  E  R  Y  Z
L  S  A  Q  L  B  M  V  C  P  R  X  Y
E  T  Q  U  P  R  I  S  C  I  L  L  A
X  H  U  F  R  O  S  T  L  U  G  S  C
Y  E  I  U  R  H  I  D  U  M  I  V  W
K  R  N  P  Y  Y  D  P  N  G  X  W  Q
L  O  O  L  A  F  L  E  G  S  P  E  D
```

51

Challenge for Session 1

God is more than we can imagine or describe. Our language about God is always short of the totality of God. We need constantly to monitor how we talk about God so that we don't limit our understanding by talking of God in the same way all the time.

In Session 1 the children learned that men and women, girls and boys, are all created in the image of God. They explored some of the many images of God that are available to us from the Bible. Some they used are God as creator (Gen. 1:26–27); one who gives birth (Deut. 32:18); rock (1 Sam. 2:2); wings of refuge (Ruth 2:12); rock and fortress (Ps. 31:1–5); shepherd (Ps. 23:1–3); stronghold for the oppressed (Ps. 9:9–10); light (Ps. 27:1); father of orphans and protector of widows (Ps. 68:5-6); potter (Jer. 18:6); hen sheltering her chicks (Matt. 23:37); and a woman who lost a coin (Luke 15:8–10).

To reinforce what they did as a group and to increase the faith and understanding of all family members, select some of the activities below to do together.

1. Create prayers for your family, using as many images of God as you can. The prayers can be for mealtimes, bedtime, the attainment of an achievement or honor such as a Scout badge, or for an important occasion such as a birthday, anniversary, graduation, birth of a child, or death of a family member or friend. Try to use an image of God that is appropriate to the prayer. For example, "Creator God" could be used for a prayer to give thanks for a new baby. "Comforter God" might be used when people are sad.

2. Take a note pad and pencil to a Sunday service of worship. Make a list of the images of God that are used during the service, including those in the hymns too. When you get home, read the list and discuss with the family the following questions: What kinds of images are there? Is there a variety? Are some of the images more masculine than feminine? Are some more feminine than masculine?"

3. We can easily get stuck in a rut with our images of God. To spark your imagination, complete these sentences with other family members:

God is like a rainbow because . . . .
God is like a kitten because . . . .
God is like the color blue because . . . .
God is like a quilt because . . . .
God is like a baseball game because . . . .
God is like a light bulb because . . . .

There are no right or wrong answers. Try having family members make up some sentences of their own.

4. One of the ways that we learn about God is through the hymns we sing when we worship God. Using a simple hymn tune, such as Old Hundredth, with family members write a stanza with images of God that are important to you. Look over the stanza. Now write another stanza with other images of God.

5. Play "Is, Is Not" in a family group. Describe each family member, taking turns as each person says what the member is and is not. For example, "Jamie is a redhead. Jamie is not bald." "Maria is small. Maria is not large." Try going around the circle describing God in this manner too.

Challenge for Session 2

We, male and female, are created in God's image and equal before God. Being created in God's image is unique to humanity. In Session 2, the children reviewed the ways we can talk about God from Session 1 and then considered the uniqueness of each person's gift of the Spirit as noted in 1 Corinthians 12:4-6. An important part of the learning was the knowledge that all persons can contribute to the work of God by using their gifts of God's Spirit.

1. Working together as a family group, write paragraphs about each member of the family. Describe the physical characteristics of the person. Include personality traits and special skills and talents. Look for the things about the person that are unique. Write in a positive manner. As the rest of the family prepares the paragraph, the person about whom the paragraph is being written can draw a picture of herself or himself. Combine the pictures and paragraphs to make a family poster.

2. Have someone read aloud to the family the following translations of 1 Corinthians 12:4–6. Discuss together: "How are they different? How does reading more than one translation help you understand the verses?"

> Now there are varieties of gifts, but the same Spirit; and there are varieties of services, but the same Lord; and there are varieties of activities, but it is the same God who activates all of them in everyone. —NRSV

> There are different kinds of spiritual gifts, but the same Spirit gives them. There are different ways of serving, but the same Lord is served. There are different abilities to perform service, but the same God gives ability to everyone for their particular service.
> —*Good News Bible*

> There is a variety of gifts but always the same Spirit; there are all sorts of service to be done, but always to the same Lord; working in all sorts of different ways in different people, it is the same God who is working in all of them.
> —*Jerusalem Bible*

3. With older children, read 1 Corinthians 12 together. In this chapter, Paul reminded the Corinthians that each one of them had a special gift of the Spirit to use in showing God's love to one another and others. Family members have special roles to play just as members of a congregation do. Talk about the role that each family member has. Ask: "How does each one contribute to the way your family works together? Are there other relatives or friends who also contribute to your family?"

4. Place a bowl or basket in a central location in your home, such as the kitchen table or a table in the living room. Near it place a pad of paper and a pencil. When anyone sees a family member use a gift or skill for the good of the family, write it down on a slip of paper and place it in the bowl or basket. After a week, read the slips together. Give thanks to God for these gifts and their uses.

5. In families it is particularly easy to assume that women and girls have one set of gifts to contribute and that men and boys have another set of gifts to contribute. For a few days or a week, list the jobs that each family member does to help all of you live together. Together with the family look at the list you have made. Ask these questions to help family members think about the ways the particular gift of each person is used. "Who does the cooking? Who does the cleaning? Who works in the yard? Who handles the family money? Who drives the car? Who decides how the money is spent?

Is there one person you think of as the boss of the family? Most of the jobs to help a family live together can be done by women, men, girls, and boys. How does each person in your family share in these jobs?"

6. Together with the family make a wall hanging to show the unique gifts of God that each family member has. Have each person think of a way to draw a picture or symbol of a gift from God that he or she uses in your family. Have the person practice drawing it on a 12" square of plain paper or a sheet of typing paper. Give each person a piece of white cloth of the same size as the paper and fabric markers or water paints to make a panel for the wall hanging. When all the panels are finished and dry, one family member can sew them together in a strip. Hang your art work of family gifts where everyone can see it daily.

We all have gifts that we can use to work for equality and justice in our community and world. To conclude this course, the children prepared a service of celebration of the gifts of women, particularly the women they studied. In it, the children also prayed that they would find ways to use their gifts to help others and to fulfill God's mission. They will need your help and support to do this.

Challenge for Session 3

In many situations and places, women and girls are not treated as equal to men and boys. We find evidence of this injustice throughout history, even in the time of Jesus, although he consistently acted against such norms of his day. In Session 3, the children heard the story of Jesus and the woman at the well (John 4:1–42) and learned about the surprising way that Jesus acted toward this woman. They also talked about ways girls and women are portrayed and treated today.

You may have begun that discussion in your family if you examined the roles and tasks each person has as suggested in Challenge for Session 2. The activities here will continue that topic and help you explore it in other avenues.

1. Do you subscribe to a magazine? Gather up some back issues. With the family look through it to see whether girls and boys are portrayed differently? Ask questions: "How many stories have girls as the main character? How many have boys? Are the girls able to solve their own problems, or must they get help from an adult or a boy? What about the boys? How are the mothers and fathers portrayed? Do the mothers work at home during the day? Are they employed outside the home? What about the fathers?"

2. Look through your local newspaper. Cut out stories that tell of inequalities regarding women or girls. Have someone read them aloud. Ask family members: "Who is working to change the unfairness? How can you contribute?"

3. Over the next week, plan to have family members watch selected programs on television to see how women are portrayed. You might want to watch a favorite program or the news show on a network for the whole week. Decide together what you will look for, such as whether a man or a woman is in charge, whether a man or a woman solves the problem, whether a man or a woman is always made to act silly or foolish, or whether men and women always do the same kinds of things or report on the same kinds of news. Have everyone make a chart to keep track of what he or she finds. At the end of the week, compare your charts. Is there anything you want to tell the television station? Remember, television producers like to hear when you think they have done a good job as well as when you think they have done something poorly.

4. Have the children talk with their grandparents or other older relatives. Then ask them, "Did any women in our family work for justice for women, such as for the right to vote?" Find out about such women. As a family, make up a skit about the woman. Join together with other families who have also made up skits. Have a potluck supper and present your skits to one another.

Challenge for Session 4

Throughout history, women have worked for others, especially in their homes and neighborhoods. In some instances, their work became more widely known. Much of this work has been as volunteers. They have often accepted these challenges because of their faith in God and have been strengthened and sustained in their work by their faith.

In Session 4, through the activity pages the children were introduced to women who fit the description above. The suggestions below will widen their knowledge of the work of women for others, as well as your own.

1. In the family group have someone read aloud the story of Dorcas in Acts 9:36–42. Ask, "Who are the women in your church and community who remind you of Dorcas?" Write thank you notes to them.

2. Ask family members, "What famous women were born or lived in your state or province? What did they do to help others find justice?" In the 1970s many women's organizations published books of short biographies of women in their area who made significant contributions to society. You or older children can look for this kind of publication in your public library. Read about one or two women. Have children write a letter to a relative who lives elsewhere or to a pen pal and tell about this woman.

3. Learn about women in your family who have worked to see that others have what they need or who have worked for the rights of women. Together prepare a list of questions to ask grandparents or great-aunts and great-uncles. If relatives live far away, send the questions in a letter. Tape the interviews or take notes or save the written responses so you have a record of this family history.

4. Create some family "holidays" honoring women who have worked in order that others might have what they need to live good lives. With family members choose a woman from the activity pages or their own research. If the woman lived near you, visit the neighborhood where she lived. Plan a project that is connected with what she accomplished. For example, if you choose Jane Addams, volunteer at a shelter for the homeless or a day-care center.

Challenge for Session 5

Some women have worked for equality and justice for all persons on a national and global basis, from biblical times until today. Sometimes they worked with that intention; in other instances their influence grew beyond their expectation or intention. In this session, the children learned about women whose influence was or is felt far beyond their communities. Perhaps you know stories about women like them.

1. Together with the family make a list of women you believe are world leaders today. Do you know how they are working for equality and justice? Select one or two women and watch for news about them on television and in the newspapers. Keep track of what they are doing.

2. Miriam, the sister of Moses, was a leader of her nation. Have someone read aloud about her in Exodus 2 as the sister who watched over Moses and in Exodus 15 as she leads the Israelite women in dancing and singing praises to God. If you have a Bible concordance, you can look up other places where Miriam is mentioned.

3. Look over the television listings for plays or documentaries about women who are working for peace, justice, and the integrity of creation. Watch them with older children. You and they can look for more information about these women in your public library.

Also watch together a play or documentary about a man. Discuss together, "What differences did you notice in the way the program was produced? What was different about the lives of the persons?"

4. Working as a family, select three women who have made important contributions to the world from the activity pages or your own research. Make a triptych (a three-sided standing picture) depicting something about their work. The background for the tryptych can be made easily from a square box. Cut off the top, bottom and one side. Use markers or crayons to draw the picture on the cardboard or on paper to glue to the cardboard.

Challenge for Session 6

1. Celebrate the gifts of your family members. Set a time when everyone can be present. Celebrate one family member on that occasion and set other times to celebrate the others. Focus on each member of your family, young and old. Give thanks for the gifts that person brings to your family. Each member can tell of times when the person being celebrated has been helpful. Serve a favorite food of the person. Say a blessing for the person. You may want to expand these celebrations to include special friends of your family. Or you might design birthday celebrations in this manner.

2. With your family learn more about your community. Find answers to the following questions: "Who are the persons who are treated unfairly? What organizations are working to get rid of unfair practices? How does your congregation help? How can it help? What can you do?" This is one way you and your child can take part in God's mission.

3. Evaluate the way your family has changed as members have participated in the challenges. Together discuss such questions as the following: "What new information do we have about the roles of women and girls? How do we see the way our congregation worships God or is organized differently than we did before? What do we know about women in the Bible that we didn't know before? How do we see one another as family members differently? What commitments do we wish to make, individually or as a family group, as a result of these activities?"

4. With the family, select a woman that you admire. Write an acrostic poem using her name. Print her name down the left margin of the paper. Write a line of poetry so the first word of each line begins with that letter of the name. For example:
   Forgotten by others, but not by her.
   Rights of prisoners were her concern
   Young and old received her care.
The lines don't have to rhyme!

Bibliography

Adult Study

Deen, Edith. *All of the Women of the Bible.* New York: Harper & Row, Publishers, 1955.

Hardesty, Nancy A. *Inclusive Language in the Church.* Philadelphia: Westminster Press, 1987.

Johnson, Suzan D. *Wise Women Bearing Gifts: Joys and Struggles of Their Faith.* Valley Forge, Pa.: Judson Press, 1988.

Moltmann-Wendel, Elisabeth. *The Women Around Jesus.* New York: Crossroad Publishing Co., 1982.

Weems, Renita J. *Just a Sister Away.* San Diego: LuraMedia, 1988.

Biographies about Women Written for Children

Forrest, Diane. *The Adventurers.* Nashville: The Upper Room, 1983.

Johnston, Joanna. *Women Themselves.* New York: Dodd, Mead & Co., 1973. Short stories, almost poetic, of 14 women ranging from the 15th through the 20th centuries.

Morey, Janet, and Wendy Dunn, *Famous Mexican Americans.* New York: Dutton, Cobblehill Books, 1989.

Turner, Glennette Tilley. *Take a Walk in Their Shoes.* New York: Dutton, Cobblehill Books, 1989. Short biographies with skits children could perform.

Cooperative Education

Johnson, David. W., Roger T. Johnson, Edythe Johnson Holubec, and Patricia Roy. *Circles of Learning, Cooperation in the Classroom.* Alexandria, Va.: Association for Supervision and Curriculum Development, 1984.

Glasser, William. *The Quality School: Managing Students Without Coercion.* New York: Harper & Row, Publishers, 1990.

Activities and Crafts

Church World Service. *Make a World of Difference: Creative Activities for Global Learning.* New York: Friendship Press, 1990.

Cray, Elizabeth. *Kids Can Cooperate: A Practical Guide to Teaching Problem Solving.* Seattle: Parenting Press, 1984.

Fry-Miller, Kathleen, and Judith Myers-Walls. *Young Peacemakers Project Book.* Elgin, Il.: Brethren Press, 1988.

Judson, Stephanie. *A Manual on Nonviolence and Children.* Philadephia: Yearly Meeting of the Society of Friends, Peace Committee, 1977.

Orlick, Terry. *The Cooperative Sports & Games Book: Challenge Without Competition.* New York: Pantheon Books, 1978.

Sing to God. New York: United Church Press, 1984.

The Great Parade

Richard Avery
Donald Marsh

"The Great Parade." Words & Music: Richard Avery and Donald Marsh. Copyright © 1971 by Hope Publishing Co., Carol Stream, IL 60188. All right reserved. Used by permission.

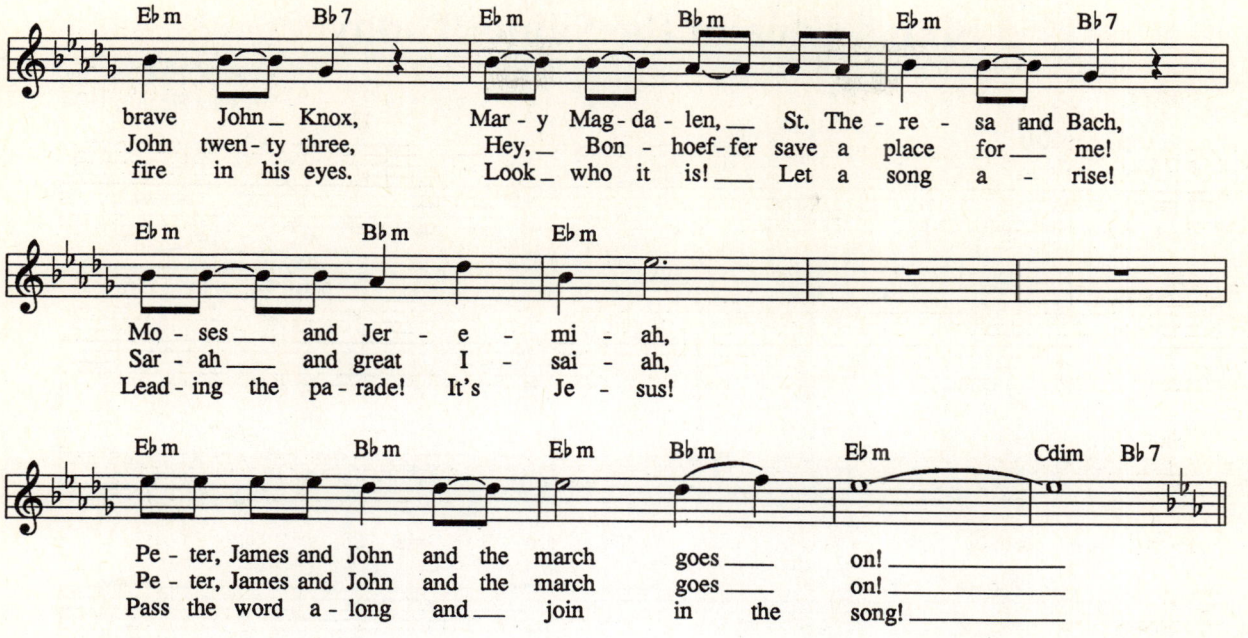

Have We Not All One Loving God?

Elizabeth W. Gale

OLD HUNDREDTH L.M.
Louis Bourgeois, c. 1510-1561
Genevan Psalter, 1551

Copyright © by Judson Press. Used by permission of Judson Press.

I Sing a Song of the Saints Today

Mary Duckert, 1974
Altered, 1979

WOODMERE, Irr.
Paul Hamill, 1974

1. I sing a song of the saints today, serving their God on earth, With deed of compassion each day of their lives improving another's worth. Now
2. Now ev-'ry one of us here was born to reflect the image of One Who created and loved us through good times and bad and sent us God's only Son. But it's

Words from *Every Tongue Confess This*. Copyright MCMLXXIV by The Geneva Press. Altered and used by permission of Westminster/John Knox Press. Music copyright © 1974 by Gemini Press, Inc. Otis, MA 01253. Used by permission.

*The word "saints" in the New Testament refers to all the followers of Jesus, not just those honored after their death for extraordinary deeds. The same may be said today.

Come, Let Us Honor Those Who Led the Way

Harriet Ilse Ziegenhals
TOULON 10.10.10.10.
Abridged from *Genevan Psalter, 1551*

1. Come, let us honor those who led the way;
   Women of Scripture witnessing each day;
   Teacher and leader, queen and prophetess,
   Through vital ministry their faith confess.

2. In years of turmoil, bitterness and pain,
   Women have sought equality to gain,
   No longer dwell upon the past with tears,
   Pledge new commitment for the future years.

3. Praise now and thanks unto our God we bring;
   Lifting each voice, with courage let us sing;
   Together we'll not from our purpose swerve,
   Building the wholeness of the Church we serve.

From *Songs of Hope and Peace*. Copyright © 1988 The Pilgrim Press. Words copyright by Harriet Ilse Ziegenhals. Used by permission.